TAKING THE VILLAGE
ONLINE

Funded by the Government of Canada
Financé par la gouvernement du Canada

Demeter Press
140 Holland Street West
P. O. Box 13022
Bradford, ON L3Z 2Y5
Tel: (905) 775-9089
Email: info@demeterpress.org
Website: www.demeterpress.org

Demeter Press logo based on the sculpture "Demeter" by Maria-Luise Bodirsky
<www.keramik-atelier.bodirsky.de>

MIX
Paper from
responsible sources
FSC® C004071

Printed and Bound in Canada

Front cover artwork: Abbigael F. Arnold, "A Mother Way to Connect," 2016, pen and ink, 5.5 x 6.75.

Library and Archives Canada Cataloguing in Publication

Taking the village online : mothers, motherhood, and social media / edited by Lorin Basden Arnold and BettyAnn Martin.

Includes bibliographical references.
ISBN 978-1-77258-082-2 (paperback)

1. Social media. 2. Motherhood. 3. Mothers. I. Arnold, Lorin Basden, editor II. Martin, BettyAnn, 1971-, editor

HM742.T34 2016   302.23'10852   C2016-905997-9

TAKING THE VILLAGE ONLINE

Mothers, Motherhood, and Social Media

EDITED BY

Lorin Basden Arnold and BettyAnn Martin

DEMETER

DEMETER PRESS

With all gratitude to those who have carried us in mothering:
to the children who have taught us through experience,
the mothers who have taught us by example,
and the partners who have taught us through love.
Thank you for being our village.

Table of Contents

III.

MOTHERS, RESISTANCE, AND SOCIAL MEDIA

Acknowledgements

Of course, there would be no acknowledgements to make without the hard work of all of the contributors to this volume, who hung in through multiple revisions and brought their experiences, intelligence, and passion for the subject to the table time and time again. We have learned much through working with these impressive scholars.

Demeter Press, and the amazing people that make it what it is, particularly Andrea O'Reilly, are owed a debt of gratitude for having faith in us to do this work and do it well, and for everything they do to promote and celebrate the study of mothering. We cannot accurately express how impactful their work has been on our lives and our scholarship.

All the mothers who have been part of our lives—including but not limited to our own mothers (Loretta Throckmartin Branson and Betty Martin), those who mothered us when our mothers were no longer with us (Kathie Basden and Joyce Hubert), our sisters, our friends, and our online relational partners—have provided role models for mothering and allowed us to learn from their successes and their challenges. We thank them for serving in that role.

And most certainly not least, we thank our life partners, Derek Arnold and Ken Paradis, for parenting with us, supporting us, helping us fill our well of parenting patience when it is running a little dry, and loving us. We truly couldn't do any of this without you.

Introduction

Mothering and Social Media: Understanding, Support and Resistance

LORIN BASDEN ARNOLD AND BETTYANN MARTIN

IN THIS ERA OF THE INTERNET, many mothers in their twenties, thirties, and forties regularly use online social media to interact with other people, including other mothers. Although mothers are sometimes criticized for spending too much time on social media (ironically, such critiques often occur on social media), they find social media to be a welcome addition to their lives.

The following text addresses social media and motherhood from a variety of approaches and perspectives. Some authors have written chapters that are fairly traditional research. Others have provided autobiographical reflection. Others still have taken their experiences using social media in working to improve the lives of mothers as a topic of consideration, and they discuss the process and impact of those efforts. Chapters here approach social media from the point of view of readers and participants and reflect a broad range of social media types, including Facebook, blogs, discussion forums, and Twitter. As the editors of this collection, we hope that this text provides a glimpse of how and why mothers use and are affected by social media, and creates food for thought regarding how social media may be used to improve the lives of mothers.

"Social media" can be somewhat difficult to define but is generally understood as an online, network-based interactive channel of communication, which promotes collaborative creation and the sharing of user-generated information (Obar and Wildman). It includes such forums as blogging, discussion forums, Facebook, Twitter, Tumbler, Pinterest, and more. Because of the pervasiveness of social media use by mothers, scholars should consider its impact on their lives. According to a study done by the Pew Research Center, 65 percent of American adults used social media in 2015, which represents a 58 percent increase in only a decade. Studies in Canada suggest similar rates, with 69 percent of the population using social media in 2013 (Canadian Internet Registry Authority). Among women, rates in the U.S. were slightly higher at 68 percent. Although young adults are the greatest users of social media, its usage has substantially increased across age groups, even for adults over sixty-five (Perrin).

The overall increase in the use of social media has also been accompanied by a small slow decrease in disparity of use based on socioeconomic factors. Income is slowly becoming less of an obstacle to access, and 56 percent of those in the lowest income brackets in the United States used social media in 2015 (Perrin). Moreover, according to the Pew study, race and ethnicity are also no longer strong predictors of use: black, white, and Hispanic adults were all found to use social media at levels greater than 56 percent. Education level is still an important variable, but that, too, is declining. In the United States, 54 percent of individuals with high school diplomas, or less formal education, use social media, whereas 76 percent of those with college degrees use it (Perrin). Thus, the use of social media is rising across diverse groups, and consequently it has begun to affect a wide range of lives and life experiences.

The Pew study does not specifically examine mothers and their usage in its study; however, other research suggests that many mothers are regularly using social media. In their 2015 study about adjusting to parenthood, Bartholemew et al. show that Facebook has become a central form of communication for new parents. The researchers found that 127 of the 154 mothers participating in the study had Facebook accounts, and 82 percent of those mothers visited Facebook weekly, with over 58 percent visiting every day (460-461). Such studies illustrate that many adults in North America are using the Internet and social media with frequency and that mothers are no exception to this trend. Little research, however, has explored the reasons for this increased use of social media among mothers and the specific needs it satisfies for them.

WHY ARE MOTHERS USING MORE SOCIAL MEDIA?

Some of the increase in social media use is related to the ubiquity of online access. Almost two-thirds of Americans own a smartphone, according to a series of studies completed by Pew (Smith). This number is near double the level of ownership found in 2011. Smartphone users have continuous access to the Internet, and in these studies, most indicate that they use it quite regularly. The availability of Internet-capable devices almost guarantees near constant access to social networks, and recent research suggests this access may be particularly crucial to mothers today.

Various scholars and theorists have argued that social support networks are important for the adjustment and welfare of parents (Bartholomew et al. 455). In past generations, mothers could count on the support of extended family members and close friends during times of maternal change and challenge. Grandparents were often geographically close, along with siblings and in-laws. They provided information about parenting and gave mothers the emotional support that they needed in order to cope with the mental, emotional, and physical demands of mothering. However, as culture has shifted to the postindustrial system, which requires less geographic stability for success and demands a more mobile workforce, this in-person support system has decreased for many mothers.

Residential mobility—the ability and tendency to relocate, sometimes frequently, across a lifespan—is a firmly rooted aspect of American culture, and it has become more common worldwide (Oishi 5). Advantages to this type of mobility include having a larger pool of career options, being able to seek a geographical location suited to a family's needs and interests, and enjoying the increased educational options that come with mobility. However, this ease of relocation also presents challenges. Patricia Drentea and Jennifer Moren-Cross argue that the increasing mobility of contemporary society, along with the reality of two-earner families, has significantly decreased traditional in-person support systems for mothers (921). Mothers can no longer assume that their friends will remain geographically close or that they will live near enough to extended family to receive instrumental, informational, and emotional support on a regular basis. Thus, mothers turn to social media forms in order to create the support networks that they now lack because of increased geographic mobility.

An additional factor that affects the use of social media by mothers is the increasing public debate about the quality of mothering based on inaccurate and problematic "mommy wars" discourse (Akass; Crowley). This rhetoric suggests that the discord between mothers who stay at home and mothers who work out of the home is vitriolic. Although such discourse tends to position stay-at-home mothering as being most consistent with the intensive (i.e., good) mothering model, and suggests that working mothers are less involved in their mothering roles, it simultaneously presents stay-at-home mothers as "inadequate in terms of their being fully functioning adults" (Crowley 219). Jocelyn Crowley and Kim Akass have argued that media representations of the mommy wars overstate the prominence of this debate in the real day-to-day interactions between mothers. The force of repetition in mediated messages, however, may create a heightened perception of division for mothers, and some mothers do find this divisiveness to be present in interactions between mothers.

The discourse of the mommy wars leads mothers to have additional feelings of uncertainty regarding their role as mothers and their place in the larger cultural system. Because mothers are positioned in mommy wars discourse as never really living up to the expectations of the culture, no type of mother can feel confident that she is following the right path. Heightening this insecurity among mothers is the lack of a face-to-face community as well as the belief that mothers cannot possibly understand or support a type of mothering different from their own. Thus, individual mothers turn to social media to find other mothers who appear to be similar to them and can provide the validation needed.

Since mothers use social media as a format to connect with other parents, what are the effects of such a use? As in any form of social encounter, the outcome is not simply a neutral exchange of information. Not only are mothers using social media, but their understandings and experiences of mothering and motherhood are being affected by it. And mothers who use social media are influencing the understandings and experiences of motherhood for others. In this book, we address three primary ways that social media affects the mothering experience.

CONSTRUCTING MOTHERHOOD AND SOCIAL MEDIA

As mothers encounter or participate in various forms of media, social and otherwise, they interact with and create representations of mothers and motherhood. As part of the fabric of social reality, these representations affect the understandings of not only mothers but of the self. In the first section of this volume, authors consider how mothers' encounters with three different types of social media—blogs, discussion forums, and the microblog format of Twitter—become part of the construction and reconstruction of motherhood understandings.

Although social media is seen primarily in terms of active participation (i.e., writing), the act of reading itself is a form of interaction and participation that can affect one's thinking. In chapter one, "Digitally Mediated Motherhood," Kate Orton-Johnson addresses the ways in which mothering blogs are experienced by mothers as readers. She considers three primary types of mothering blog posts that mothers see and read, and discusses how those interactions are processed by mothers in terms of their understandings of self and others.

Multiple motherhood scholars have considered the use and value of online forums for mothers (Arnold; Drentea and Moren-Cross; Pedersen and Smithson), as this form of social media has become frequently used by mothers seeking community. In chapter two, "The 'Wicked Stepmother' Online," Kristi Cole and Valeri Renegar examine the narratives of stepmotherhood and stepmothering expressed by participants in an online bulletin board. Using Kenneth Burke's concept of the "terministic screen," they consider how the negative framing of the stepmother role can prevent stepmothers from developing positive understandings of themselves; moreover, such a negative framing can potentially have negative effects on the relationships between members of blended families.

The microblogging format of Twitter lies in an interesting space of social media—somewhere between a blog and an online forum. The limits on message length on Twitter create both opportunities and challenges for users, but participants have used it to create connections, share life experiences, participate in political discussions, market businesses and products, and even attempt to challenge cultural ideologies (Dixson; Pamelee and Bichard; Potts). In chapter three, "Confession in 140 Characters," Lorin Basden Arnold looks at the microblogging platform of Twitter and how mothers represent themselves and their mothering performance in the form of 140-character tweets. She considers the ways in which tweets denoting "bad mothering" can function to reinforce, question, or challenge ideologies of motherhood.

SUPPORTING MOTHERS THROUGH SOCIAL MEDIA

Social media is not only a vehicle for the construction and reaffirmation of understandings of mothering but also a mechanism for supporting mothers in their role (Arnold; Drentea and Moren-Cross). As we discussed previously in this introduction, mothers turn to social media to seek support when they feel that their face-to-face community cannot provide what they need. The support may come in a variety of forms, including informational and emotional support. In section two of this volume, authors discuss the ways in which social media can be leveraged to create opportunities for supporting specific communities of mothers and the challenges present in such efforts.

Breastfeeding is a topic of controversy in some arenas but is highly beneficial for both mothers and infants (Anholm). However, the act of nursing is not without challenge, and mothers often require support to have a positive experience with nursing. The absence of a support community can be particularly common for some populations, including military personnel and their families. In chapter four, "Boobs, Babes, and Boots," Amy Barron Smolinski discusses Mom2Mom Global, a nonprofit organization designed to provide breastfeeding support to military moms. As the executive director of Mom2Mom, Smolinski explains why support within the military population is needed and outlines the organization's successful mechanisms used for to support nursing mothers.

The reliance of mothers on social media for support is similarly reflected by Leah Williams Veazey. In "Mothering in the Digital

Diaspora," she considers how mothers who are separated from their social networks by geographic disjuncture use social media to locate and create relationships with others. With increasing internationalization of the workforce, more mothers find themselves separated not only from family and friends but also from their home cultures, including all of the associated cultural beliefs and understandings about family. Veazey's work explores the use of both closed Facebook groups and open blog networks as ways of linking expatriate mothers, and examines the way that each can provide support for mothers who feel isolated.

During pregnancy, a large number of mothers experience unplanned Caesarean births, which can have a poor effect on the health and welfare of mothers and their children (Goer et al.; Lowe). However, social support can help mothers reduce those negative outcomes. In chapter six, "Mothers of Honor," Tara Stamm, Casey Yu, and Stephanie Kennedy discuss their experience with maternal "paying it forward" though social media to create communities of mothers who provide support to mothers who have experienced traumatic births.

Many examples of support efforts for mothers and mothering online relate to the provision of support from mother to mother through the creation of voluntary relationships facilitated by for-profit or nonprofit organizations; however, the digital format also provides opportunities for formal structured parenting education work. In chapter seven, "Mothering is Not a Game," Amy Cross discusses a pilot project using game-style virtual worlds to conduct parenting classes. She argues that many mothers may be reluctant or unable to attend in-person mothering classes because of the potential stigma related to taking such classes, the difficulty of arranging childcare, and the trouble securing transportation to the classes. Thus, online courses using social media forms, such as an avatar-based chat space, can present valuable opportunities for mothers.

MOTHERS, RESISTANCE, AND SOCIAL MEDIA

Giving and receiving support or information are not the only ways mothers can and do engage with mothering via social media platforms. From blogs to Twitter to Facebook and beyond, social media has become a prominent mechanism for resistance to cultural hegemonies of various types (Cook and Hasmath; Mclean and Maalsen; Penney). The performance of "outlaw" mothering (O'Reilly) is taken up in the final section of the book, as the contributors consider some of the ways in which mothers intentionally engage in efforts to challenge the power of intensive mothering hegemony.

In chapter eight, "'From 'Fakebooking' and 'Flaming' to a 'Moms' Support Network,'" Bronwen L. Valtchanov, Diana C. Parry, and Troy D. Glover examine the ways in which a social media environment can repress or promote resistance to the intensive mothering ideology. They address the specific factors of the fee-based private site *momstown.ca* that cause mothers to experience it as a more supportive forum for resistance than they have encountered on other discussion boards or on Facebook. While mothers in this study use *Momstown* to seek support, they simultaneously resist culturally enforced standards of good mothering.

More specifically engaging the idea of conscious resistance, chapters nine and ten extend O'Reilly's conception of the "mother outlaw" into the social media frame. In "Hip Mama," chapter nine, Anitra Goriss-Hunter examines the series of websites connected to *Hip Mama*, and addresses the ways in which its structure and style facilitates the creation of a resistance discourse. In chapter ten, "Virtual Outlaw," Jocelyn Craig connects the mother outlaw to the digital world in her examination of feminist mothering groups. Both authors consider not only the ways in which mother outlaws attempt to resist hegemony of mothering, but also the ways in which the pull of celebrated understandings of motherhood can create resistance to resistance.

Finally, in chapter eleven, "Feminist Parenting Online," Meika Loe, Tess Cumpstone, and Susan B. Miller use a multimethod study to address feminist parenting represented by blogs and the ways in which blogs provide starter sites for resistance that can move into offline communities. They consider the benefits of feminist mother blogging to the writers and to the community of readers, as well as the obstacles encountered in the attempt to engage feminist principles through this form of social media.

Participating in online forums, Facebooking with friends and family, Tweeting about the challenges of mothering, supporting mothers through virtual reality, and blogging about resistance to accepting models of maternity—these are only some of the ways that mothers use social media forms to meet their needs in a technology-focused world. As the world shifts and changes, communication opportunities and challenges arise and are enfolded in the conversational stream of mothering. Communication about and between mothers on social media represents a different forum for the creation of new motherhood understandings and motherhood enactments through conversation. What is most unique about this new way of interacting is the sheer volume of opportunity mothers have for stepping into the stream of motherhood conversation and deciding whether to move with or against the prevailing current.

WORKS CITED

Akass, Kim. "Motherhood and Myth-Making: Dispatches from the Frontline of the U.S. Mommy Wars." *Feminist Media Studies*, vol. 12, no. 1, 2012, pp. 137-141.

Anholm, Cheryl Hancock. "Breastfeeding: A Preventive Approach to Health Care in Infancy." *Issues in Comprehensive Pediatric Nursing*, vol. 9, no. , 1986, pp. 1-10.

Arnold, Lorin B. "10 Years Out—Presence and Absence in a Long-Term Online Mothers' Community. *Motherhood Online*, edited by Michelle Moravec, Cambridge Scholars Press, 2011, pp. 73-97.

Canadian Internet Registry Authority. "Canadian Internet Forum—2013 Report." *Canadian Internet Registry Authority*, CIRA, 2016, https://cira.ca/node/9246. Accessed 3 Sept. 2016.

Cook, Julia, and Reza Hasmath. "The Discursive Construction and Performance of Gendered Identity on Social Media." *Current Sociology*, vol. 62, no. 7, 2014, pp. 975-993.

Crowley, Jocelyn E. "Unpacking the Power of the Mommy Wars." *Sociological Inquiry*, vol. 85, no. 2, 2015, pp. 217-238.

Drentea, Patricia and Jennifer Moren-Cross. "Social Capital and Social Support on the Web: The Case of an Internet Mother Site." *Sociology of Health & Illness*, vol. 27, no. 7, 2005, pp. 920–943.

Goer, Henci, et al. "Vaginal or Cesarean birth: What is at Stake for

Women and Babies?" *Transforming Maternity Care*, National Partnership for Women and Families, 2013, transform.childbirth-connection.org/wp-content/uploads/2013/02/Cesarean-Report.pdf. Accessed 1 May 2016.

Lowe, Nancy K. "The Overuse of Cesarean Delivery." *Journal of Obstetric, Gynecologic, & Neonatal Nursing*, vol. 42, no. 2, 2013, pp. 135-136.

Mclean, Jessica, and Sophia Maalsen. "Destroying the Joint and Dying of Shame? A Geography of Revitalized Feminism in Social Media and Beyond." *Geographical Research*, vol. 51, no. 3, 2013, pp. 243-256.

Obar, Jonathan A., and Steve Wildman. "Social Media Definition and the Governance Challenge: An Introduction to the Special Issue." *Telecommunications Policy*, vol. 39, no. 9, 2015, pp. 745-750.

Oishi, Shigehiro. "The Psychology of Residential Mobility: Implications for the Self, Social Relationships, and Well-being." *Perspectives on Psychological Science*, vol. 5, no. 1, 2010, pp. 5–21.

O'Reilly, Andrea. *Mother Outlaws: Theories and Practices of Empowered Mothering*. Women's Press, 2004.

Pamelee, John H., and Shannon L. Bichard. *Politics and the Twitter Revolution: How Tweets Influence the Relationship between Political Leaders and the Public*. Lexington Books, 2011.

Pedersen, Sarah, and Janet Smithson. "Mothers with Attitude: How the Mumsnet Parenting Forum Offers Space for New Forms of Femininity to Emerge Online." *Women's Studies International Forum*, vol. 38, 2013, 97-106.

Perrin, Andrew. "Social Media Usage: 2005-2015." *Pew Research*, Pew Research Center, 8 Oct. 2015, www.pewinternet.org/2015/10/08/social-media-usage-2005-2015-about-this-report/. Accessed 1 May 2016.

Potts, Amanda. "Exploring 'Success' in Digitally Augmented Activism: A Triangulated Approach to Analyzing UK Activist Twitter Use." *Discourse, Context, & Media*, vol. 6, 2014, pp. 65-76.

Smith, Aaron. "U.S. Smartphone Use in 2015." *Pew Research*. Pew Research Center, 1 Apr. 2015, www.pewinternet.org/2015/04/01/us-smartphone-use-in-2015/. Accessed 1 May 2016.

I.
CONSTRUCTING MOTHERHOOD
AND SOCIAL MEDIA

1.
Digitally Mediated Motherhood

Mommy Blogs and Reading Mothering

KATE ORTON-JOHNSON

DIGITAL TECHNOLOGIES HAVE OPENED UP new environments in which the experiences of motherhood and mothering are narrated and negotiated. As such, online spaces
have become important domains where stories of motherhood are
articulated. Researchers have long theorized the complex identities
and expectations associated with practices of mothering. Similarly,
the emerging literature mapping the digital terrain of motherhood
points to the often-contradictory ways that the Internet can liberate and constrain. During times of transition—characterized by
geographic or social isolation, identity transformation, and new
unfamiliar demands—digital social networks provide solace, support, and social capital for mothers (Drentea and Moren-Cross;
Madge and O'Connor; Moravec). However, these same spaces
are also sites of conflict, where stories, identities, and practices of
mothering are contested and redefined (Leavitt).

In this chapter, I use the example of "mommy blogs" to reflect
on these contradictions and present an analysis of the ways that
digitally mediated stories of "doing" motherhood are consumed
and understood by their readers. I outline a typology of mommy
blogs and explore the ways in which mothers (re)construct their own
narratives and understandings of mothering through their reading
of these blogs. This focus on the *consumption* of blogs contributes
to a body of research on digitally mediated motherhood that has
focused primarily on the ways that those actually engaged in the
practice of blogging experience the digital spaces and relationships
that they create (Friedman). Although rich empirical detail exists

on bloggers self-expression and collective identification (Friedman and Calixte; Webb and Lee; Moravec), researchers have paid less attention to how the kinds of motherhood represented in mommy blogs are consumed and interpreted by mothers who define themselves as "readers" rather than active bloggers. In this sense, the lived reality of these readers, and the ways that this reality interacts with digitally networked narratives of motherhood, has been rendered invisible. Accordingly, in this chapter, I explore how blogs can reveal new ways of thinking about the social and cultural construction of the identity of mother and the "doing" of motherhood though a continuum of online and offline spaces and interactions. I argue that blogs act as a meso level between the experience of mothering at an individual or micro level and the expectations and understandings of motherhood at a cross-cultural or macro level.

BLOGGING, MOMMY BLOGS, AND THE MAMASPHERE

Blogs as a mainstream form of online and popular culture are well established, and mommy blogs as a genre describe the practice of writing online accounts of motherhood and family life. In sharing experiences of motherhood through networked life writing, bloggers have created a collective of maternal narratives commonly referred to as the "mamasphere" (Friedman). Mommy blogs are usually informal and personal in tone and there is often the implication that they provide a no-holds-barred approach to documenting family life. Although the main focus of many mommy blogs is motherhood and children, the mamasphere represents a diverse and often disparate range of voices. Mommy bloggers write about a range of topics, from politics to popular culture, and have been defined as radical and responsive to the dominant discourses of motherhood; they provide a multidimensional view of motherhood and of life in a private-public sphere (Peterson).

Debates about the nature of the mamasphere and digitally mediated maternal subjectivity highlight the complexities and controversies surrounding the term "mommy blogging," which both compliments and demeans (Lopez). Mommy blogs celebrate the personal as political but also reinforce the domestic identity and status of the mother. Mommy blogs are positioned as sites of female activism and rebellion (Peterson), but at the same time, they conjure up well-worn social and cultural judgements about mothers as "apron-clad sycophants to their tiny sovereigns" (Friedman and Calixte 25), which reflects the enduring gender politics conferred by the title "mom."

Although questions about the nature and politics of the mamasphere remain, there is little doubt that web 2.0 technologies, such as blogs, have created a wider public sphere in which motherhood is represented and, importantly, a space in which dominant discourses of motherhood are challenged, negotiated, and redefined (Bradley; Lopez). In articulating diverse, ambivalent, and candid narratives of mothering, mommy bloggers create and sustain spaces that contribute to contemporary constructions of parenting as a cultural ideology. The identities and practices of mothering are (re) constructed and (re)produced in particular socioeconomic, cultural, temporal, and—I want to emphasize here—technological contexts.

Thinking beyond blogs as primarily supportive communicative spaces is central to understanding these technological contexts. The mamasphere is not simply the visible voices of bloggers and commenters. Audiences or readers of blogs also interact and engage with these representations and use them in their own (re) constructions and (re)productions of mothering. These audiences have been implicit, but often invisible, in debates about the meaning and significance of the mamasphere. This is an important omission. While some blogs have small audiences of only friends and family members, many blogs achieve international popularity (Ley) and, given their interactive possibilities, are important spaces in which meanings of motherhood are consumed and debated. The more mundane and invisible ways that technology shapes constructions of motherhood are made visible by considering the consumers or readers of blogs that do not define themselves as web-2.0 "active" but, through their lurking, are engaging in meaningful ways with these narratives.

CLASSIFYING THE MAMASPHERE

This chapter examines data from research with thirty-two mothers about online representations of motherhood and their consumption of digital content. All of the women regularly read mommy blogs but did not write blogs. Eighteen of the mothers who participated in the study responded to notices about the research that I posted in a range of online mothering forums and Facebook groups. The remaining fourteen participants responded to notices placed in doctor's surgeries, toddler groups, public libraries and community centres. Interviews with the mothers were conducted face-to-face, over Skype, and by email, and all of the respondents participated in at least two interviews that often included "reading breaks"— when they directed me to particular blogs or blog entries that they wanted to discuss. A strong theme emerging during the fieldwork was the way in which, as consumers of mommy blogs, mothers were active in classifying and categorizing the blogs that they read. Mothers sat with me with their laptops, tablets, or smartphones and talked me though the various blogs that they followed and their reading strategies; some blogs were read daily, some weekly, and some more intermittently. The respondents had very clear ideas about the range of different voices represented by mommy blogs and had active strategies for seeking out and avoiding certain blogs types in different contexts.

During the research a typology emerged of mommy blogs, and for the purposes of this chapter I will focus on three key blog types: intensive blogging, reality blogging, and confessional blogging. This typology is in no way exhaustive and does not assume that a blog is static, consistent or uniform. Blogs shift focus and they may encapsulate more than one type. But the categorizations outlined here follow the ways in which the mothers, as readers, managed and ordered the breadth of voices in the mamasphere. In this way, the typology represents a continuum of practices that reflect the diversity of blogs and the diversity of ways that they narrate the experience of motherhood.

INTENSIVE BLOGGING

The first type of blog identified represents what has been broadly defined in academic and media debate as the ideology of intensive parenting, where the mother is held primarily responsible for a process of childrearing that is child centred, emotionally absorbing, and labour intensive (Hays). Here, the blog performance of motherhood fits with normative expectations of motherhood as easy, natural, and fulfilling (Lee).

These blogs explore aspects of domesticity and wellbeing seen as central to the identity of mother. Blog entries focus on health and fitness, healthy eating, home management and organization, home renovation, raising good children and good citizens and maintaining familial stability and emotional health. Often entries emphasize the value of creativity as part of family life, the teaching of lost skills and crafts as a rejection of mass production, and crafting as a personal and personalized part of childrearing: As Anne[1] explains:

> One blog that I love to hate has this woman going on about making bunting or pompoms or some essential home decor for ever[y] conceivable occasion. Then it all matches the wholesome snacks she will serve at whatever it is being celebrated, a kids birthday, Halloween, the fact it's Tuesday. Sometime I feel myself being drawn into it all and think that I'm going to carve melon balls into dinosaur eggs and then I remind myself who I am—not this Stepford mum.

For Anne, the narratives of motherhood presented in this kind of blog are cultural scripts that she wants to resist. But even in resisting the narratives—"I remind myself who I am"—she is engaging with representations of certain kinds of motherhood.

What is at stake here is not the cultural and structural politics around the nature of different kinds of parenting; rather, these narratives, even when resisted, play into the proliferation of "mommy wars" and the pursuit of an unattainable lifestyle, as Louisa suggests:

> A type of blog that I find particularly exhausting, on many levels, is the one that has clearly bought into the whole "modern parent" thing. Everything is perfect; there are crafts and well-rounded meals and perfectly packed school bags lined up the evening before. Despite knowing that

what they are spouting is nonsense and knowing that this is clearly not really what this woman's life is like, I find myself, if not buying into it, then wondering how they are juggling and balancing all these things when I'm clearly not and not wanting to. I frustrate myself reading them but like a moth to a flame, I constantly am.

In reading and mocking these type of blogs, the mothers reflect on their practices of parenting and navigate their own understandings of motherhood in opposition to a narrative that they recognize as constructed and performed—one that they try to resist but one that still casts a shadow of unmet expectations. The consumption of this kind of blog raises some interesting questions about notions of reality and authenticity that parallel the typology of blogs that emerged. The intensive blogs were not seen by the participants as realistic representations of motherhood and were perceived as airbrushed ideals that mask the more chaotic and disordered reality of mothering that they experience.

REALITY BLOGGING

In contrast to blogs representing the intensive mothering ideal, the second type of blog was defined by the participants as documenting the reality of family life portrayed in all of its messy mundanity. Stories of picking up and dropping off children at school and nursery, household finances, children's sleeping or eating problems, and sibling rivalries present the unpolished antidote to representations of the perfect mother and the perfect family across a range of other blog types and mainstream media.

Posts were characterized as "a day in the life stuff," and readers noted that these kinds of blogs often explicitly positioned themselves as spaces of validation and comfort ("if you're looking for perfection and homemade crafts you won't find them here"[2]) and as a way in which to share frustrations and commiserations ("here is where you can find honesty about the challenges of being a mother"). In this sense, the practices and daily routines of mothering played out across the mamasphere rest on assumptions about mommy blogs as a communicative, sharing, and interconnected collective. Blogs act as spaces where bloggers and their readers can find solace, comfort, and solidarity with someone whose experiences are similar to their own. In fact, readers of reality blogs felt particularly challenged by these narratives and by their own consumption of the everyday stories, as Lisa states:

> I often wonder why these bloggers aren't just in forums just talking to other mums. But then why don't I just talk to other mums? Why am I reading about other people's dull stuff just so I can see if I am feeling the same? I want to say "get a life" but then here I am reading them. I think I like these ones best when I just want the equivalent of someone saying "yup, me too."

The blogs were frequently defined as dull and reasons for reading them were related to a cathartic need to find a more realistic view of motherhood. Importantly, this was not about making connections or communicating with other mothers in any way beyond reading the blogs. Few of the respondents ever commented on posts, but they maintained that the blogs' presence alone was sufficient and, as Claire suggests, the blogs were used as a symbol that provides a sense of sharing and conformity without the need for any emotional work or expectation of reciprocity:

> One the one hand I am mocking these uber-mums [from intensive blogs] while feeling a little like I could and should do more, then I'm going to the boring old blogs that fit more like slippers. The nosy bit of me likes being reassured that day-to-day family life rumbles on for all of us, and I don't have to pressure myself to run a marathon while breastfeeding and home schooling and looking fabulous in order to be doing ok. I don't want to talk about it and hash it all out with friends when I can just read the solidarity.

In this sense, the simple act of reading was a valued way in which mothers engaged with wider debates about mothering practices. Mothers identified with digitally networked narratives of motherhood but took on a spectator role more closely associated with models of traditional media consumption. Blogs were seen as "real" domestic soap operas that provided an insight into the ways that seemingly banal but authentic practices of mothering could be shared.

CONFESSIONAL BLOGGING

The third type of blog develops this notion of authenticity and reality by presenting a more subversive version of motherhood that uses sarcasm and humour, and frequently courts controversy. By far the most commonly read and popular type of blog among my sample, confessional blogging of the "bad" or "slummy" mommy type has been positioned as a backlash to the narratives of maternal perfection. Challenging the good mother myth, these blogs represent rebellion against and rejection of idealistic and utopian version of motherhood presented on mainstream and social media (Blanchett; Peterson).

Confessional blog posts are characterized by maternal failings, self-depreciation, and "true tales" of horrible or embarrassing motherhood experiences. Rather than celebrating the joys of parenthood, confessional blogs focus on techniques to get through the day until it's "wine o'clock," outlining parenting "fails" or "cheats," and discussing boredom, frustration, and deficiencies.

Although some argue that the confessional tone employed by these "bad mother" bloggers points to an expectation of judgement about inadequacies and failures (Yonker), they can be read as a celebratory genre that relishes the status and label of subversive and rebellious, As Victoria argues:

> There is as much debate about the "bad" mother blogs as the overly polished perfect mother blogs. I think it's been embraced as a liberation, and it's become a place in which people are saying what not so long ago would have been utterly taboo, you know, "my daughter is a bit of a bitch," but using clever humour, and as a reader, it's a whole other way of thinking about you as a parent and human.

For these mothers, consumption of confessional blogs is about humour and release, and the blogs provide a space in which recognition is given to the challenges and complexities of the role of the mother and, importantly, to the limitations of conventional representations and cultural understandings of this role. As Janey explains:

> I'm trying to think of how, pre these kinds of blogs, this kind of conversation would unfold or where you would find them. You'd have to know people pretty well to admit some of this, but I think this whole huge [confessional] blogging thing, even though it's exaggerated and sometimes just clearly done to shock, it opens the floodgates. Just them being there goes a long way.

The readers find value the humour in these blogs, even while acknowledging that these types of blogs are as performative and unrealistic in their representations of motherhood as the intensive parenting blogs that they critique, which allows them to engage with their own, often conflicting identities as mothers and women.

WHAT IS THE USE OF READING BLOGS?

The brief typology I have outlined here speaks, to some extent, to the ways in which the mamasphere is a communicative space in which mothers can exchange information, tell stories, confide fears, and as a result of these interactions and connections, they can find empowerment and social capital that can be transformative for their experiences and understandings of motherhood. However, the definition of this collective needs to expand to include those who are not active in terms of community building or in fostering friendships but who are "active lurkers" (Orton-Johnson). For these readers, the use of the blogs is about the selective consumption of familiar spaces, in which certain aspects of motherhood are being shared and articulated in sympathetic ways. This active selection is akin to what Michelle Moravec describes as the creation of spaces in which mothers can move beyond binary choices of self-sacrifice or self-recrimination (xiii) As Sian states:

21

> I think the main thing for me is that I can go to the blog that represents the kind of mother I am being today. I know that if I want support that the writing and the comments and responses to that writing of a particular blog will do that job of making me feel that it's not just me and it will be ok, if I'm "bad" mother, "trying to find a rainy day craft" mother or just "need to know someone else does the same" mother.

This sense that that mamasphere is a flexible and fluid space allows for a definition of digitally mediated community that includes the presence and power of those lurking and invisible, for whom blogs also create a sense of engagement and belonging. These readers use blogs and engage with them in ways that are meaningful to their own practices of mothering. This is important, as by representing a plurality of modes of motherhood outside of those in the mainstream media, blogs provide their audiences with a foil or mirror through which identities are validated, negotiated, reconsidered, and rejected. Jennifer articulates the process in the following way:

> It's not providing me with "community" or "support" in the ways that one might imagine—you know, "frazzled new mum finds great friends online"—but it is providing a sense of solidarity, like the blogs are a backdrop to my motherhood that I reply on as a space to breathe and feel like the experience is shared.

The plurality of the mamasphere also enables readers to create their own bricolage of mother identities, and in navigating this myriad of voices they find a continuum of practices and narratives that contextualizes, challenges, and reinforces their understandings of their own mothering practices.

In this way, blogs serve an important role in acting as a middle ground or as a meso level between macro constructions and representations of motherhood—in popular culture, policy initiatives, state and political apparatus, and societal institutions—and the micro level of interpersonal relationships and individual choice.

This meso level is important for bloggers, not just in the ways outlined in the literatures relating to community and support (Drentea and Moren-Cross; Madge and O'Connor; Moravec) but also for the more passive consumer of these spaces, who defined themselves as "only" readers but are able to access a range of voices and experiences.

Conceptualizing the mamasphere as a meso level of interaction and experience is important in the context of understanding the Internet as ubiquitous and routine in contemporary lives. As Christine Hine argues, the Internet is embedded, embodied, and everyday: embedded in a range of "offline" activities, embodied in the ways in which people engage with the world, and every-day in its mundanity and invisibility (19). Applying this logic to the mamasphere, critical attention should be paid to the ways in which representations of motherhood and mothering in blogs are not confined to the space of online activity but in fact shape and inform motherhood activities, practices, understandings, and emotions. Blogs are situated in a wider multimodal and multimedia landscape and digital ecosystem. They connect with and flow through Instagram accounts, Facebook pages, Twitter feeds, and a range of social media that creates a complex digital footprint of motherhood. As Hine argues, being online occurs alongside and compliments other ways of being and acting in the world, and the ways people interact with the internet are embedded in multiple frames of meaning, motherhood being one.

There are complex issues at play here that pose interesting questions about the nature of motherhood, identity and of storytelling in a digital era. Web-2.0 activities of interaction take place across a range of platforms; consist of producing and consuming digital spaces of parenting; and create a digital footprint that represents different ways of articulating the "doing of motherhood" and the cultural construction of the identity of mother. Accordingly, in talking about contemporary narratives of motherhood, these are spaces and interactions that warrant further investigation, particularly the less visible articulations and engagements with the mamasphere outlined in this chapter. The Internet, and the mamasphere in particular, provides a forum for the broadcasting of women's voices, the community to support and condemn those voices, and a backchannel of mothers navigating and reflecting on those voices. Scholars needs to pay critical attention to the visible and invisible ways in which digitally mediated social, cultural, and technical constructions of motherhood are being played out constructed and consumed in the mamasphere. More importantly, given the embedded, embodied, and everyday nature of the Internet (Hine), researchers also need to reflect on the ways in which the mamasphere is in a reciprocal relationship with the day-to-day lived experiences and practices of motherhood in potentially transformative ways.

NOTES

[1]Pseudonyms are used throughout the chapter to protect the identity of the participants.

[2]These examples are paraphrased as exemplars from the sample of blogs studied.

WORKS CITED

Blanchett, Aimee "The Rise of the 'Bad Mom' in the Social Media Age." *Star Tribune*, 22 Jan 2015, www.startribune.com/bad-moms-backlash-women-brush-off-social-media-perfection/289336021/. Accessed 10 Nov. 2015.

Drentea, Patricia, and Jennier Moren-Cross. "Social Capital and Social Support on the Web: The Case of an Internet Mother Site." *Sociology of Health and Illness*, vol. 27, no. 7, 2005, 920-943.

Friedman, May. *Mommyblogs and the Changing Face of Motherhood*. University of Toronto Press, 2013.

Friedman, May and Shana Calixte, editors. *Mothering and Blogging. The Radical Act of the MommyBlog*. Toronto: Demeter Press, 2011.

Hays, Sharon. *The Cultural Contradictions of Motherhood*. Yale University Press, 1996.

Hine, Christine. *Ethnography for the Internet: Embedded, Embodied and Everyday*. Bloomsbury Academic Press, 2015. Print.

Lee, Christina. "Social Context, Depression and the Transition to Motherhood." *British Journal of Health Psychology*, vol. 2, no. 2, 1997, pp. 93-108.

Ley, Barbara. "Beyond Discussion Forums: The Transmediated Support Culture of an Online Pregnancy and Mothering Group." *Motherhood Online*, edited by Micjelle Moravec, Cambridge Scholars Publishing, 2011, pp. 23-43.

Lopez, Lori. "The Radical Act of "Mommy Blogging": Redefining Motherhood through the Blogosphere." *New Media and Society*, vol. 11, no. 5, 2009, pp. 729-747.

Madge, Claire, and Connor, Henrietta. "Parenting Gone Wired: Empowerment of New Mothers on the Internet?" *Social and Cultural Geography*, vol. 7, no. 2, 2006, pp. 199-220

Moravec, Michelle, editor. *Motherhood Online*. Cambridge Scholars Publishing, 2011.

Orton-Johnson, Kate. "The Online Student: Lurking, Chatting, Flaming and Joking." *Sociological Research Online*, vol. 12, no. 6, 2007. *Research Gate*, doi: 10.5153/sro.1615.

Peterson, Emily. "Mommy Bloggers as Rebels and Community Builders: A Generic Description." *Journal of the Motherhood Initiative for Research and Community Involvement*, vol. 6, no. 1, 2015, jarm.journals.yorku.ca/index.php/jarm/article/view/40238. Accessed 22 Aug. 2016.

Webb, Lynn. and Lee, Brittney. "Mommy Blogs: The Centrality of Community in the Performance of Online Maternity." *Motherhood Online*, edited by Michelle Moravec, Cambridge Scholars Publishing, 2011, pp. 244-257.

Yonker, Madeline. "The Rhetoric of Mom Blogs: A Study of Mothering Made Public" Dissertation, Syracuse University, 2012.

2.

The "Wicked Stepmother" Online

Maternal Identity and Personal Narrative in Social Media

KIRSTI COLE AND VALERIE R. RENEGAR

THE STEPMOTHERING ROLE IS BOTH a product of contemporary culture and an evolution of the traditional mother role. Although stepmothers differ vastly in their experience and their role in families, there has been little progression in the popular framing of stepmothers. Instead, the term has become embedded in an interpretive frame that reifies stereotypes of the "wicked stepmother" or "step-monster" and ignores all other possibilities. There are few alternative frames and no compelling ones for understanding the way that stepmothering exists in popular culture. Unfortunately, unless the biological mother is dead or dying, the stepmother is largely framed as negative. The circulation of the stereotypes surrounding stepmothers' impact affects not just popular culture but the online discourse about and by stepmothers in social media. In particular, online discussion boards serve as a rich text through which to understand how stepmothers respond to and use the language that frames their familial role. In this chapter, we argue that the consistent negative framing of this role, understood in the context of Kenneth Burke's "terministic screens" (45), directs attention away from the ways that stepmothers contribute to the dynamics of contemporary families and limits their identities to popular characterizations that range from selfish and uncaring to malevolent. The lack of competing terministic screens to understand and describe stepmothers constructs a linguistic trap in which the odds are stacked against the success of the stepmothering relationship with children, with spouses, and in the larger social network of relationships both on and offline.

26

Mothering holds a sacred place in American culture; however, stepmothers are largely castigated by the public mind. The maternal role, as socially constructed and performed, has been a growing subject of feminist scholarship. A uniquely interdisciplinary endeavor, motherhood studies is the focus of researchers in such fields as psychology, economics, sociology, history, rhetoric, and gender and women's studies. However, with the exceptions of some research on the stepmother in fairy tales and the economic or psychological impact of blended families on children, the figure of the stepmother is not well represented in this research. The invisibility of the stepmother is significant, particularly because 50 percent of the sixty million children under the age of thirteen in the United States are currently living with one biological parent and that parent's current partner (Vespa et al.). Thus, exploring the rhetoric that constructs stepmothering illuminates how stepmothers are able to frame their identity within the prevailing terministic screens in online discourse. As stepparents and rhetorical scholars, we are acutely aware of the different type of motherhood that we experience and the ways in which it is socially constructed by the larger mothering culture. According to Lindal Buchanan, mothering culture constitutes a "slippery terrain," in which the biological, social, psychological, economic, legal, and ideological collide (xvii). If motherhood studies are a fraught site of exploration, examining stepmothering is exponentially so because of the larger cultural stereotype that circulates about stepmothers. And although motherhood studies in the field of rhetoric and communication studies have gained significant traction in the last decade, this work tends not to adequately address the role of stepmothers.

The language used in popular culture to describe stepmothers frames the attention of American culture in particular ways. Burke indicates that our language creates a "terministic screen" that "directs the attention into some channels rather than others" (45). This means that particular language choices and characterizations shape an understanding of the things that they describe. Furthermore, both those who make these linguistic choices and the audiences who hear them are encouraged to direct their attention to certain features of what is being described while other aspects of what is being described are cast into shadow or made less noticeable.

Burke explains, "Even if any given terminology is a *reflection* of reality, by its very nature as a terminology it must be a *selection* of reality; and to this extent it must function also as a *deflection* of reality" (45). A terministic screen, therefore, focuses attention on particular characteristics by bringing them to the forefront, whereas more complex or nuanced understandings of the subject at hand are far less prevalent. In the abbreviated language of online discussion boards, the direction of participant attention towards only certain features is all the more pronounced. Paul Stob summarizes Burke's thinking, "terms direct our attention, goading us to notice some things at the expense of other things" (139). Not only does a terminology direct attention in particular ways, but it also has embedded within it particular conclusions. Discussing the "nature of our observations," Burke explains, "much that we take as observations about 'reality' may be but the spinning out of possibilities implicit in our particular choice of terms" (46). From this, we argue that the repeated circulation of the "wicked stepmother" or "step-monster" representation highlights particular negative aspects of the stepmother. Because these terms are so prevalent in American culture, the terministic screens that they create make it difficult for individuals to consider stepmothers or stepmothering without first thinking about the way that they have been negatively framed. We argue that the constant repetition of the "step-monster" and "wicked stepmother" tropes in popular culture, including social media and online environments, poison the meaning of "stepmother" and the relationships that it describes. In a finding that suggests the possible effect of these embedded conclusions about stepmothers, a three-decade longitudinal study indicates that children often come to appreciate having a stepfather but the relationship with the stepmother is more difficult and resentment is more intense (Martin 3). In other words, the prevalence of the negative terministic screens surrounding stepmothers resonate with the difficult and resentful relationship that many children report having with their stepmothers. The negative terministic screen provides a lens for describing stepmothers in ways that then replicate and entrench the negative framing.

As a product of the language and culture that create them, terministic screens have the power to direct attention in particular ways, but they can also be deliberately cultivated to create new perspectives and meaning. Carefully examining terministic screens also illuminates how those with different interests and different vantage points characterize events from their shifting points of view (Hawhee 134). As individuals use language to describe the reality that they experience, the repetition of particular characterizations over time creates and reinforces terministic screens. Language, then, shapes values and understood realities. As Burke argues, through communication, humans produce individual and social change (qtd. in Hawhee 135). Thus, the stereotype of the wicked stepmother helps to create a frame of understanding that devalues those women who marry someone with children as it simultaneously reinscribes the value of "real" mothers. Challenges to this stereotype are made more difficult by the sheer gravitas of the cultural value placed on biological motherhood (McQuillan et al. 481). In a cycle of reinforcement, the negative framing makes it difficult for stepmothers to forge positive relationships with their stepchildren and the children's biological mother, which then reinforces the general cultural misunderstanding of stepmothers. As stepmothers struggle against the dominant cultural representations of themselves, they turn to social media in an attempt to understand their own mothering experiences. On the discussion boards, they tend to start from the assumption that they are communicating with audience members who are negative about their parental role, even when interacting directly and, in the case of the board we analyzed, only with other stepmothers.

However, terministic screens are not fixed. They evolve and change as language, assumptions, and values shift over time. Terministic screens are reflexive in that they are both shaping perspectives at the same time that they are being shaped by perspectives. As literary or linguistic conventions gain traction in popular discourse, they become increasingly dominant and powerful in terms of their construction of meaning. This is true in online communities as well as in face-to-face communities. Nicole Brown argues that the terms that exist within online communities shape the participants' understanding of a particular community while that community is constructing and shaping the way it is described (Brown 93). Thus, language is part of a reflexive process and, consequently, should be approached critically and rhetorically (93). In the analysis that follows, we explore a sampling of stepmothers' self-descriptions in the online stepmothering community in order to better understand the way in which the community and the participants co-construct one another.

The omnipresence of the "wicked stepmother" stereotype shapes public understanding of the role of stepmothers and sets family members up in a fraught position in which the experience of having a stepmother and the experience of being a stepmother are presumed to be negative. Mavis Hetherington and John Kelly, the author of the longitudinal study, report that "many of her subjects described their stepmothers as 'evil, malevolent, wicked, or monsters' and gave them nicknames like 'Dog Face' and 'the Dragon'" (Hetherington 193). In American culture, Wednesday Martin argues, "Disliking stepmothers is easy; suspecting them is more or less automatic. Caring about stepmothers, expressing concern about what they are going through, considering their reality at any length- all of this requires a leap of faith. Even by women with stepchildren themselves" (Martin 6). Martin's "leap of faith" is a useful metaphor to pursue in terms of thinking beyond the wicked stepmother; however, in the context of Burke's terministic screen, it is also nearly impossible, even for stepmothers themselves. As Martin notes, "once we have gotten to the place of caring a little less about how others view us, once we have decided, on some level, to focus our hopes in directions other than winning his kids over no matter what it takes and put our energies elsewhere, we sometimes refer to ourselves with knowing smirks as 'step-monsters'" (10-11). Instead of spending time and energy embroiled in the guilt of being the un-mother, some successful stepmothers, at least according to Martin, adopt the term "step-monster" for themselves as a way to reframe their experiences. We argue, however, that even the attempt to reclaim a negative term simply reifies the screen through which cultural and social expectations shape experiences within and reactions to blended families.[1]

In order to begin an investigation of stepmother identity, we turned to social media and to online discussion boards. There, we sought the voice and perspective of stepmothers to discover the ways in which they understand and construct their identities as they negotiate their experiences in blended families. We analyzed posts in the largest stepmothering discussion board of the popular parenting website *babycenter.com*. The board "Step Parents *The Original*" was created on 13 March 2008 and to date has 6,883 active members. With over 240,000 comments since its inception, it is the most active board on *babycenter.com* related to stepmothering. We analyzed the posts by moderators and stepmothers from 1 September 2014 to 15 October 2014 to discern the terministic screens that shaped the conversation about stepmothering.

Before discussing the posts in detail, we highlight the welcome message that is pinned, or permanently available, at the top of the discussion board.[2] The welcome message not only outlines the most common family formations within the blended family ("We have SPs [Step Parents] of all kinds here: custodial, noncustodial, 50/50, long distance - you name it"), it also reifies the possible experiences of the stepmother by defining predictable categories: high conflict situations, adjustment, venting, and difficulty. Although the welcome message is ostensibly about support—"We're here to listen, offer support, and give the benefit of our experiences. You're not alone"—it also amplifies the negative frame for the stepmother while clearly delineating the thematic categories that we identify below. The welcome message starts with an expectation of isolation and then transitions to the inevitable threat experienced by the stepparent in relationship with their stepchildren: "Remember, our active posts may show up on the BBC [BabyCenter] main page, and we certainly do not want to perpetuate the "wicked stepmother" stereotype in the eyes of the casual lurker." Thus, the possibility for criticism from the audience is immediate in the online space as a lurker, an individual who is not a member of the online community, may interpret a stepmother's parenting struggles as indicative of her wickedness. The moderator also assumes that competition with the birthmother is inevitable. "Support and kind advice most often does not include the words, 'look at it from BM's [birthmother] perspective.' Those words are often insulting and unhelpful." The stepmother experience is being foregrounded, but there is the explicit assumption that others will respond by defending the birthmother perspective. This sentence, then, suggests that the stepmother's perspective is not as valuable as the viewpoint of the birthmother and indicates that, in the world of parenting, the mother's perspective is of paramount concern. The moderator continues, "We do ask, however, that non SPs respect that this is a SPs' group by not coming here purely to vent about dads and SMs/SPs [stepmother-stepparents] or to discount a SP's plight." "Plight," an unfortunate or difficult situation, then is the defining characteristic for describing the experience of the step-parent. In using a term that defines stepparenting as a dangerous or precarious situation, the welcome message frames the situation for people in blended families and, thus, shapes the realities of the relationships for people in those families. These are the rules for the board, and they function as the grammar that participants have to follow in order to use the board. The welcome message reinforces the terministic screen for the emotions that participants feel and the experiences that participants have; this is the borderland of the stepmother. In other words, this board is not a place of wellbeing and contentment; it is not a space for sharing the experience of satisfaction for a parenting job well done. It is a place to vent about fraught relationships and the myriad ways in which those relationships are discordant.

For this analysis, we coded 55 posts out of 172 made in the one-month period.³ Posts were included in the analysis if the stepmother explicitly discussed her role in the family. We iden-tified the following themes in the discourse: guilt, competition with the birthmother (BM), competition with the children, and marital conflict. Additionally, regardless of the general theme of the post, the stepmothers frequently invoked the stereotype of the "evil" stepmother and consistently characterized stepmothering as unpleasant and isolating.

Beginning with the welcome message on the board warning against the perpetuation of the wicked stepmother stereotype, a majority of the posts that we examined include the terms "wicked," "evil," "monster," "bad person," or "witch." For example, a poster on 1 October 2014 writes, "Are there are other parents out here who can help me feel less like a wicked stepmother whose DSD's [Dear Step Daughter] are going to resent us forever?" Another participant on 13 October writes, "I'm sure I am portraying myself as the ugly wicked stepmother here, but I'm not trying to be," as she questions whether or not it is okay for her to feel hurt that her stepson does not want to hug her. In addition to affection, small issues tend to provoke stepmothers to question their actions within the context of being wicked or evil, as a post from 18 September reveals: "I at least tried to get him to eat healthy at our house. Not super healthy but at least some fruits and veggies like grapes and corn.... I became seen as the wicked step mother even though I loved this kid and only wanted what was best for him." Some active participants use the wicked stepmother language to set up juxtaposition between themselves and other women. In a post from 4 September, a participant writes, "What can I do? I don't like being frustrated at the situation towards them, but he has got to help and realize I'm not trying to be mean or an evil step mom. (I grew up with a true evil step mom so I know that I am not one)." To invoke the "true evil step mom" allows this participant to distance herself from that stereotype while simultaneously participating in the terministic screen that reinforces it.

In addition to using language consistent with the public image of stepmothers as bad, these posts also overwhelmingly suggest that stepmothering is both difficult and lonely. In their messages, stepmothers include apologia about their feelings of frustration, confusion, or anger that affect their ability to parent. The admission of stepmothering being deeply difficult is included in almost all of the posts that we sampled. For example, in a post on 11 September 2015, a participant writes "I don't know why I have so much difficulty with this, it's frustrating. I just want to accept it, adjust well, and stop stressing about it cause it's not going to change. I have no one to really talk to about it because no one in my social circle is a step mom, so they just don't get it." As this stepmother indicates, the experience of stepmothering can be emotionally challenging. Furthermore, stepmothers may feel unable to share their experience with stepparenting because they fear others will not understand. Thus, the experience of stepmothering can be insular.

The feeling of isolation is a significant factor in the predominance of the "evil" stepmother construction because stepmothers tend not to be surrounded with a community of support or others who can counter the overriding cultural understanding of stepmothers. The online community provided by this discussion board would seem to provide stepmothers with this support. However, based on the comments in these posts, the guiding stereotype of evil or wicked is alive and well. Additionally, the difficulty and isolation of stepmothering can reify the embedded conclusion of the term, as the challenges begin to feel as if they result from a flaw in the stepmother. In this way, the conclusion that stepmothers are wicked or evil becomes a seemingly supported reality for the stepmother. In turn, guilt about her role in the family may become a dominant driver in a stepmother's understanding of herself and her relationship with her stepchildren.

The guilt theme is prevalent when understood through the terministic screen of the wicked stepmother or step-monster. Guilt plays a prominent role in how the participants on the board describe themselves. A participant posting on 1 October 2015 reflects, "I am not proud of this but I can't stand being in my home with my two young stepchildren.... They are not misbehaving that much and I feel like a monster for feeling this way." This participant refers to both the monster and the guilt. With no social cues beyond the monstrous, the defensiveness of stepmothers towards one another is commonplace in these posts. "What im going to say next people might think im a bad person but their [sic] my feelings and are [sic] trying to deal with them." These women, like many social media users, participate in the boards seeking a place to vent, confess, or connect with others in an attempt to understand their experiences. They seem uncertain regarding the construction of their own identity as stepmothers because this role is not well defined or understood in society and in the family, and the isolation they feel compounds this uncertainty. Another 1 October participant asks, "Am I a bad step mom? ... Am I wrong to feel this way?" In these posts, the participants denote the fundamental construction of stepmother: "bad" and "monstrous." The constant questioning about being bad at their new parenting jobs and the assumption that even other stepmothers will chastise them for their feelings contribute to an enhanced sense of guilt. Guilt is a frequent theme on the stepparenting board. The phenomenon of wishing away the stepchildren and the guilt associated with that feeling is recurrent, particularly in cases in which the stepmother is parenting the children of a birthmother with whom she experiences conflict.

Competition with birthmothers is the second most common theme in the examined posts. On these boards, it is rare that stepmothers do not assume that the birthmother is attempting to undermine their relationships with the children. One post plainly states, "Dear BioMom ... I am not a 'step monster' ... Stop trying to make me look bad!" The fear of being undermined, of having an already tenuous relationship destroyed by the jealousy or anger of the birthmother, is a recurring theme. On 5 September 2015, a participant writes, "I have not taken away from her that she is the mother and I've never tried to 'take her place' besides taking over what she's failed to do." The power of the birthmother culturally and the role she often plays in a blended family constructs the stepmother's response to her role: "Honestly, I'm just tired of hearing her name. It's like we can't get rid of her. She constantly comes up in conversation and it just feels like we can't live a normal life." This post from 11 September 2015 is particularly telling, because the stepmother views the existence of the birthmother as an impediment to normalcy. The stepmother is expressing frustration about the ways that the presence of the birthmother in the remarriage and blended family creates competition. Conflict with the birthmother, however, is difficult to manage when children begin to pick up on the tensions in the blended family. Although stepmothers can do their best to ignore the possible things said by the birthmother, it is infinitely harder to ignore the ways that the children manifest the tension resulting from the conflict between the birthmother and stepmother. As one participant writes: "Every memory of me is blocked out and she [the stepdaughter] only brings up things with her mom. Or she says: I went there with my mom (but it was me). Like she blocks me out." We interpret the replacing of the stepmother as a function of the normative cultural narrative of mothering that erases the stepmother entirely. Competition with the birthmother forces the children into an untenable position, which continually affects the relationship with their stepmother: "The negative associations I used to tie to DSS [Dear Step Son] about BM were quite unfair and about my unresolved feelings about parenting another's child and, I'm going to admit it, my insecurity." The stepmother experiences "insecurity" because her identity has been negatively constructed. Any attempt to renegotiate that identity is a risk—an act of individualism that defies and potentially reconstructs given meanings and limitations on the performance of prescribed roles. Although conflict and competition with the birthmother may be troubling, it is less shameful for stepmothers than feelings of competition with the children.

Competition with the children may be the most dominant stereotype surrounding the stepmother in popular culture, and it is certainly just as common in this sample as conflict with the birthmother. The trope of the wicked stepmother in Disney movies, for example, is grounded in the usually fatal competition between the stepmother and her female stepchild, which is a manifestation of the stepmother's supposed hatred for the child. Of course, although terministic screens frame stepmothers as villains, the lives of stepmothers today are hardly Disney movies, and stepmothers are not actually wicked witches, so when this stereotype is paired with guilt over their conflicted feelings towards the children, competition typically manifests itself as a love-hate dichotomy towards the children. "I can't stand my stepson. I love him ... OMG I love him. But literally, just being in the same room with him these last ... ten months, I cringe." The adoption of the motherly "OMG I love him" is meant to offset the expression of negative feeling that this stepmother has around her stepchild. The author's construction of this post mirrors the language that biological mothers may use to describe their dichotomous feelings about parenting. Mothers love their children, but they can be frustrating and infuriating. Time spent with the children is not time spent alone or with a spouse. This love-hate dichotomy is no different than the kinds of dynamics that would happen in a nuclear family. However, the love tie of biological mothers is culturally assumed and, thus, dilutes the power of negative feelings. For stepmothers, there is not the same assumption of maternal love to buffer conflicted feelings and feelings of competition with the children for the father's time or affection. The posts on the discussion board illustrate that stepmothers feel this love-hate dichotomy with the children, but that there is no language to express these feelings that is not characterized as petty or evil.

When the conflict over an uncertain parenting role takes up so much time and emotional space, the resulting anger, guilt, and jealousy (often not communicated to the spouse) frequently result in serious marital conflict. According to studies done by Shaunti Feldhahn and Tally Whitehead, and Mavis Hetherington and John Kelly an estimated current divorce rate of stepfamily couples is roughly between 45 and 50 percent, and a projected divorce rate is roughly between 50 and 60 percent (Deal). A 2010 study of over fifty thousand stepfamilies found that the top five categories most predictive of marital happiness were: personality compatibility, communication, conflict resolution, shared leisure, and couple flexibility (Deal and Olson). The discussion board tends to feature stepmothers whose marriages do not seem to be successful, since these categories for happiness are rarely expressed by stepmothers when describing their relationships, particularly communication and conflict resolution. Although marital conflict takes many forms, it may be understood, in part, as the result of both competition with the birthmother and resulting tension with the children: "I have to admit, I used to get jealous seeing DH [Dear Husband] parenting DSS." In this post, the normative state of parenting incites jealousy and guilt. The uncertainty generated by these emotions often leads the stepmothers active on the board to engage in polling. The most common poll is whether or not stepmothers would choose to become stepmothers again: "If you had to do it over, would you marry someone with children? 97/113 no." Every few months someone asks the question, "Would you do it over?" As represented by the poll from October 2015, 85 percent of stepmothers active on the discussion board indicated that they would not remarry their spouse. On 25 September, a participant writes, "my DH asked me today if I could take everything back and never had met him if I would. I said "no I wouldn't" but deep down inside I thought "Hell YES! I wish I would have never met you."

Ironically, the fact that these partners are communicating with one another about their relationship sets them apart from other members of the board. Typically, the participants indicate that they are too angry or resentful to broach the conversation within the marriage, so they turn to the board. Posts suggest that this resentment and anger frequently manifests itself in one of two ways. First, the birthfather may not parent in the way that the stepmother prefers, and the different parenting styles create a chasm: "Stuff like this makes me aggravated all the time with SS. It's put a wedge between us. I really shouldn't be mad at him. I really should be mad at husband for teaching him His actions were ok." This kind of comment is typical of posts regarding anger over spousal parenting style. The second way in which marital conflict presents itself on the boards is through confessions that outwardly reinforce the wicked stepmother screen: "I always look and feel like bad cop/evil stepmom while my SO [Significant Other] is a good cop and king daddy to his kids." Such posts suggest that these mothers believe the terministic screen of evil stepmother is affected how the children perceive them, which creates stress in the marital relationship.

This glimpse of a stepmothering discussion board demonstrates some of the tensions embedded in the ways that we understand the relationship between women and the children of a remarriage. Motherhood is a site of conflict that vacillates between lived experience, embodiment, and cultural expectations. The term "mother" is a rhetorical construction constantly negotiated, contested, and lauded in in American society. We have argued that the concepts associated with the term "stepmother" both reify and depart from the commonplaces of the mothering experience. Through these associations, the label "stepmother" functions as a terministic screen precluding the possibility of a positive familial relationship. Examining the ways that our terministic frames limits these relationships is an important step in understanding the specific shared experiences that Martin calls the "stepmother reality" (5). It is clear from the discursive conventions surrounding stepmothers culturally and socially, and from the experiences of stepmothers who communicate online on this discussion board, that this particular terministic screen dominates. However, the power of a terministic screen is culturally negotiated, and the capacity to reconstruct labels, roles, and identity is only limited by the ability to imagine them differently. Rethinking current terminology may destabilize the screens used for describing the stepmothering role and allow new descriptions to emerge, particularly in social media, as it moves so quickly. To put it simply, a new term and a resulting new terministic screen are needed, through which to understand nonbiological mothering. We do not have a concrete solution to this problem, but we believe that this research is one of the first steps to understanding what stepmothers are up against. It is unfair to families, children, and parents to set stepmothers up for failure by embracing and circulating a terminology that often constructs them as "wicked" or monsters. As members of our culture have more conversations about what to call this role and how to more fairly and accurately characterize it, we argue that an alternative term should capture the importance of the role, its level of responsibility, and the unique nature of this close-caring relationship, while also avoiding competition with biological mothers.

We are both stepmothers, and in the course of discussing alternative terms for this role, we realized that our experience of naming in the stepmother relationship is similar. Kirsti's six-year old stepson has always referred to her as "my Kirsti" when introducing her; Valerie's stepchildren call her "Valie," a nickname that they created and no one else uses. Similarly, the seven-year-old referred to her as "my Valie." This sense of ownership is notable. "My ___" delineates the relationship as unique, but the addition of the first name also marks it as personal. We find this parallel structure of the possessive with our proper names telling. In both cases, our stepsons were very young when we entered their lives—under two years old. Instead of using the name of the role (i.e., stepmom-stepson) our stepchildren have used our names as descriptions, not only of who we are but also of *what* we are to them. Our names take on the significance of the parenting role but with a unique connection to our children. And by mirroring that construction back to them, using the possessive with their proper names, we have somehow managed thus far to circumvent the awkward use "step-", which has spared the children having to explain something that at their ages, they do not yet understand. Additionally, by removing a form of "mother" from our title, we have removed any sense of competition with the biological mother and have simultaneously avoided a lesser-than kind of motherhood. We are not "step" or "mother." Instead, we are someone's unique and personal person. With such a new term, one that functions beyond the terministic screen of the wicked stepmother, it may be possible to shift the assumptions guiding the relationships between stepparents and their children for well over thirty million children in the U.S. It may be possible to approach a nonbiological mothering relationship without guilt and resentment. It may also be possible to reconfigure dialogue related to normative family dynamics to fit the statistical reality of family structures in the twenty-first century.

NOTES

[1]Although there are examples of individuals or groups that have reclaimed negative terms and repurposed them for positive ends, this tends to be most effective when a term has fallen out of popular use.

[2]All quotes were taken from this website: http://community.baby-center.com. For the message board, see community.babycenter.com/post/a52548100/go_welcome_message_-_board_rules_and_guide-lines.

[3]Although this board is meant to be inclusive of stepparents across the gender spectrum, it is worth noting that all of the posts sampled were from self-identified stepmothers in heterosexual pairings.

WORKS CITED

Brown, Nicole R. "'Community' Metaphors Online: A Critical and Rhetorical Study Concerning Online Groups. *Business Communication Quarterly*, vol. 65, no. 2, 2002), pp. 92-100.

Buchanan, Lindal. *Rhetorics of Motherhood*. Southern Illinois University Press, 2013.

Burke, Kenneth. *Language as Symbolic Action*. University of California Press. 1966.

Deal, Ron L. *The Smart Stepfamily: Seven Steps to a Healthy Family, Revised & Expanded Edition*. Bethany House Publisher, 2014.

Deal, Ron L., and David Olson. *Remarriage Checkup, The: Tools to Help Your Marriage Last a Lifetime*. Bethany House Publisher, 2010.

Feldhahn, Shaunti, and Tally Whitehead. *The Good News about Marriage: Debunking Discouraging Myths about Marriage and Divorce*. Multnomah Books, 2014.

Hawhee, Debra. "Burke and Nietzsche." *Quarterly Journal of Speech*, vol. 85, no.2, 1999, pp. 129-145.

Hetherington, E. Mavis and John Kelly. *For Better or For Worse: Divorce Reconsidered.* W.W. Norton and Company, 2002.

Martin, Wednesday. *Stepmonster: A New Look at Why Real Stepmothers Think, Feel, and Act the Way We Do.* Houghton Mifflin Harcourt, 2009.

McQuillan, Julia, et al. "The Importance of Motherhood Among Women in the Contemporary United States." *Gender & Society*, vol. 22, no. 4, 2008, pp. 477-496.

"Step Parents The Original." *Baby Center—Community*, Baby Center LLC, 2016, http://community.babycenter.com/groups/a25355/step_parents_the_original. Accessed 12 Aug. 2016.

Stob, Paul. "'Terministic Screens,' Social Constructionism, and the Language if Experience: Kenneth Burke's Utilization of William James." *Philosophy and Rhetoric*, vol. 41, no. 2, 2008, pp. 130-152.

Teodorescu, Adriana. "The Blog as an Instrument of Deconstructing the Mass Culture Stereotypes of Postmodern Motherhood: Two Case Studies." *Echinox Journal*, vol. 28, 2015, pp. 156-170.

Vespa, Jonathan, et al. "America's Families and Living Arrangements: 2012." Open file report, U.S. Census Bureau, American Community Survey, 2011.

"Welcome to Our Step Parents." *Baby Center—Community*, Baby Center LLC 2016, http://community.babycenter.com/post/a52548100/go_welcome_message_-_board_rules_and_guidelines. Accessed 23 Aug. 2016.

3.
Confession in 140 Characters

Intensive Mothering and the #BadMom Twitter

LORIN BASDEN ARNOLD

I N THIS NEW ERA OF COMMUNICATION, social media forms have allowed mothers and other family members to move beyond historical patterns of negotiating the meaning of motherhood mostly through face-to-face conversation. As evidenced throughout this volume, blogs, Facebook, online forums, and other forms of Internet discussion have provided mothers with new venues for working through their own understandings of motherhood and mothering. With its limit on length of post, relatively anonymity, and unrestricted viewing, Twitter provides an interesting and unique context for discussions of mothering.

In this work, I examine discussions of mothering on Twitter, written by mothers, with a focus on the concept of "bad mothering." Although Twitter has become a popular outlet for challenging societal gender expectations (Dixson 39), I argue that construction of the bad mother on Twitter is primarily confessional rather than openly transformative and, generally, represents a reinforcement of the intensive mothering model. However, within that general pattern exists a subtle but persistent resistance against the intensive expectations of motherhood.

INTENSIVE MOTHERING

In 1996, Sharon Hays wrote a persuasive and insightful text analyzing the unacknowledged outcomes of the dominant conception of mothering in North America, which she labelled "intensive mothering." This viewpoint defines good mothering as making all decisions from the subject position of the child, and positions the maternal obligation as the creation of a happy and secure childhood that will lead to a successful adult life. Mothers performing their maternity from this viewpoint are highly emotionally and physically connected to the child and set aside their own needs and desires in order to understand those of the child.

As revealed by a variety of mothering authors in Linda Ennis's 2014 text, *Intensive Mothering: The Cultural Contradictions of Modern Motherhood*, this understanding of mothering still persists. Although mothers may understand the enactment of intensive mothering differently, scholars (Johnston and Swanson 517; Christopher 91-93; Arnold 61; Huisman and Joy 101-102), have found that mothers consistently recognize the priority placed on following basic intensive mothering concepts, including the importance of the mother in a child's development, the primacy of responsiveness to child needs, and the attention to the innocent and precious nature of the child. This model of good mothering appears in public discourse across media forms, including online considerations of mothering.

TWITTER

As a form of "microblogging," Twitter provides an interesting combination of anonymity and mass distribution with small bites of information. Although there are similar platforms, such as Instagram, Twitter remains the most popular space for microblogging. According to the company, thirty-two million users are active on Twitter each month ("Company: About"). These users create a staggering amount of discourse occurring in 140-character "tweets." Users may elect to follow other users, which gives them notice of each tweet sent; may view tweets about "trending" topics; or may search for tweets related to issues or people of interest.

Given the sheer number of tweets that occur in any single moment, the use of hashtags (#) is a common tactic for Twitter users to indicate the subject of a tweet. Hashtags provide a convenient mechanism for linking tweets about common topics; they can be used to create and maintain communities of users united around a common interest, and they are also used as a shorthand way to make metacommentary about the content of the tweet (for example, the hashtag #sarcasm tells the reader how to understand the message). As argued by Leslie-Jean Thornton (49), the use of a hashtag indicates that the subject of the tweet has an elevated worth, something that is deserving of a larger conversation. Thus, to hashtag a subject rather than simply writing about it implies that the writer believes others share an interest in the topic and have a shared meaning regarding it. Through this mechanism, the Twitter user specifies an imagined audience (Marwick and Boyd 130; Zappavigna 211) to which he or she can direct the tweet. Michele Zappavigna argues that hashtags then play a role in performing identity by creating affiliations with a larger community of individuals with some shared identity, which calls out a set of understandings held by or about that community (212).

LOOKING AT #BADMOMS

For this analysis, I followed hashtags related to "bad" mothering for a period of sixty days. The selected tags used were #badmom, #badmommy, and #badmother. I removed all tweets that contained pornographic images or links to pornographic images and videos from the data set because these posts rarely contained any text. A set of 819 tweets with these three hashtags remained for analysis. Of the full data set, 12 percent represented tweets related to "mothering" of pets, and five 5 percent of the tweets addressed issues connected with inanimate objects (e.g., a purse). Of the remaining discourse, 18 percent of the tweets discussed the mothering of others. Because my focus considered how mothers represent and enact their own identity relative to these labels, I did not include those tweets in the final analysis. In the end, I considered 65 percent of the total data set, or 533 tweets, from mothers using the #badmom-related hashtags to label their own enactments of mothering. Within that data pool, I identified four consistent intensive mothering supportive themes: bad mothering as happiness harm, bad mothering as excessive self-focus, bad mothering as a failure of maternal devotion, and bad mothering as inappropriate emotional response to mothering. Additionally,

I found one theme that suggested resistance to the "bad mother," whether through more implicit challenges via humuor, irony, or questioning, or through explicit rejection of the label.

THEMES OF THE BAD MOTHER ON TWITTER

Happiness Harm

One common idea invoked in tweets with the #badmom hashtags is that bad mothers are mothers who do things that make their children unhappy. The unhappiness is at times significant, but often it is the distress a child may experience over minor things. How this unhappiness occurred fell into three general areas: failure to fulfill the child's desires, deliberate cause of child distress (or not attempting to relieve it), and accidents or other uncontrollable events that led to unhappiness.

Mothers on Twitter identify their own behavior as being "bad" when they are unable to fulfill their child's desires or have not acted in a way that would fulfill those desires.

> I told my kids that the ice cream truck driver only takes cash. I saw that he has the Square now.[1] SSsshh! #Badmommy

> So my daughter has decided she wants to be Lambie from Doc McStuffins for Halloween ... only everywhere is sold out. #badmom

Although such disappointments as these are seemingly small, it is telling that they are big enough not only to be posted on Twitter but to also be labelled as an example of bad mothering.

Some mothers posted about incidents in which the happiness harm is a source of humour for them, yet the use of the hashtags indicates that they should not enjoy the child's discomfort, even if the child is ignorant of such humour.

> I put Halloween decorations up, that always helps scare them to sleep. Muahhhh! #BadMommy

> I like to announce that I'm glad it's Friday so I can Netflix

and chill, just to see the looks of horror on my children's faces. #BadMom

Playground accident rendered Sagan sobbing & bloody-nosed.
"Worse. Day. Ever!!" he wailed. Tried (failed) not to laugh. #badmom

These posts suggest that humour at the expense of the child is understandable and a shared parental experience, but it is not a characteristic of society's expectations of good mothering.

The happiness harm theme is not limited to situations in which mothers caused unhappiness for the child or found joy in an uncomfortable or unhappy moment. The most common type of happiness harm mothers wrote about on Twitter involved incidents when an accident or a compulsory event (such as going to school or getting a physical exam) created distress for the child. These events, largely out of the control of the mother, justify the label of bad mother.

Man my baby's skin is so sensitive. I kissed him & I didn't think that my lipstick would make his skin react ... but it did. #badmommy

Awh I just accidentally made Tripp puke from having the hiccups after laughing so hard. #badmommy

Ellie went after her big bouncy ball, bounced off it, and fell backwards onto the sidewalk. CRACK! #nobloodthistime #2ndinjurytoday #badmom

I totally betrayed my baby yesterday by letting the evil nurse inject him not once but three times. #badmom #ifeelhorrible #hehatesme

In all of these situations, mothers have labelled themselves as "bad" because of the child's unhappiness, regardless of the fact that there was little the mother could have done to prevent it.

Although these are varied examples, they all represent situations in which the intensive mothering focus of consistently seeking or creating happiness for the child has somehow been violated. Intent appears to matter little in these tweets. What is important is that the mothers have not kept the child happy. Even though mothers, in some cases, express their own laughter or pleasure at the unhappiness of the child, they simultaneously invoke the #badmom label, which suggests their awareness that such a violation is inappropriate.

Excessive Self-Focus

Mother performance can be seen as subpar not only when children are rendered unhappy but also when mothers behave in ways that suggest they may be prioritizing themselves rather than focusing on the needs and desires of the child. Although this can be seen in a variety of forms, the most common types of posts were instances of mothers not prioritizing the mother persona, and focusing too much attention on their own needs, desires, and interests.

Women who mother occupy a variety of social role spaces simultaneously. They are individual adults, with the cultural freedoms and expectations attached with that role. They are women, with the gender demands associated. They are often spouses or partners. They are also mothers. Although this is the case, the intensive mothering model promotes an identity enactment whereby other roles become less important than the mothering role and are set aside completely in the presence of the child.

Because one important aspect of the mothering role is to raise the child to be a well-socialized member of the culture, mothers are expected to model the best adult behaviour at all times in front of children. Thus, behaviour that is acceptable, but possibly not ideal, for adults is not acceptable for mothers.

My 4 year old will be getting in trouble for new cuss words at preschool tomorrow. #Royals #TakeTheCrown. #badmommy

I swear my 13m old has said "shit" 3 times today ... well, shit. #BadMom #MomLife #Toddler

Helping the girl with her religion homework. Drinking wine. #badinfluence #badmom

Even when the concern is not about modeling behaviors seen as inappropriate for children, mothers still judge themselves as bad for not enacting the mother persona at all times.

My swear jar could finance the f@cking space program. #PottyMouth #BadMommy

How can I still be hungover ... from Friday?! #BadMom

I myself turn into a ten year old boy anytime Uranus is mentioned. Boys and I have way too much fun joking about it. #badmom?

Although acting in non-mother-like ways can be seen as a sign of a bad mom, that is not the only way that mothers can be understood as devoting too much attention to themselves. Simply by paying attention to their own needs, interests, or desires, mothers perceive themselves as engaging in poor mothering. Mothers who designate themselves as #badmoms for focusing too much on themselves are often, though not always, displaying (apparently inordinate) interest in the consumption of either food or media.

And the worst mother award goes to: Me. I keep eating my son's teething cookies. #ashamed #badmommy

i been waiting for my daughter to go night night so i can eat without sharing **evil laugh** #BadMommy

#badmommy moment ... getting so into the articles and news. almost forgot to go get kids from school! #elxn42 #canadavotes

The children are getting a long-awaited new video game today, so I will be reading. I'm gonna read so hard my eyeballs fall out. #badmommy

I'm in trouble. I ate all the strawberries and didn't save Junior any. #Badmommy #oops #mommyfail

I told baby "Scandal's on" and she said "night night" and walked over to her crib. Good Baby. #badmommy #scandal

Examples such as these were plentiful in the sample. In these tweets, mothers identify behaviour that indulges their own desires as inconsistent with good mothering practice.

Whether being a bad example to the child, acting in ways that are not representative of the mothering role, or pursuing individual desires and needs, tweets that represent the excessive self-focus theme are violations of the intensive mothering expectation of always prioritizing the child's needs and desires. Mothers writing these tweets mostly are not apologizing for the behaviour; instead, they are confessing, sometimes gleefully, that they have violated the expectation.

Failures of Maternal Devotion

Even when not particularly focused on the self or causing express harm to a child's happiness, mothers can still assess their behaviour as a failure to show adequate levels of devotion to the tasks of mothering. Tweets of this nature tend to fall into two general categories: mothering absence and mothering work not completed.

As the intensive model of mothering is predicated on a continuous awareness of the child's needs and desires, it calls for mothers to be available constantly. Issues related to maternal availability are at the root of the so-called mommy wars, and it is not surprising that mothers negatively evaluate themselves when they are unable to be present for their children.

I totally bailed on back to school meeting tonight. #Bad-Mommy. [Husband] went

I was up at 4 so I overslept this morning and missed saying goodbye to my kids on their first day of school. #badmom

Missed the whole comp because I am working #badmother

but I have been cheering him on from afar.

Gracie has just Skyped me in tears over #1dsplit. Her first heartbreak & I'm at work 1000s of miles away. #badmother #sacrifices #mummymedic

I am the worse mom ever. I forgot I had to pick up my kid at Cross Country practice and stayed later at work. #isuck #iforgotmykid #badmom

As can be seen in these examples, mothers on Twitter chastise themselves for not being present for their children regardless of the reason. Many of the tweets about being absent were due to work obligations, but that did not prevent mothers from characterizing themselves as bad, terrible, or even "the worst."

The most prominent category failure of maternal devotion was tweets that confessed to mothering work that was not completed. Although the tasks or obligations invoked could often be performed by mothers or fathers, the use of the #badmom hashtags suggests that these mothers understood the work to be theirs and not performing it to be a mark of poor mothering. Tweets related to not performing mothering duties included failures in teaching children, feeding the family, and keeping the house.

2nd kid starts preschool ... and I forget to take pictures :). #badmommy #MOTY #fb

I forgot to play tooth fairy last night. #badmommy

Woke up late and misses the bus on the first day of school. Brilliant. At least she wasn't tardy. :X. #badmommy #itstooearly #school

I had to use the #chickfila card already on the second day of school. #badmom

So... Clara's birthday is in like 2 weeks and I have planned NOTHING. #badmom

> I'm such a great mom. 10yo: My gym clothes are supposed
> to be washed once a week.
> You washed mine once. #parenting #badmom #parentingfail

Such tweets indicate that some mothers on Twitter believe that
certain household tasks—which include documenting the life of
the child, preparing homemade dinners, and laundry—remain the
domain of mothers and that mothers who do not complete those
tasks have failed to adequately fulfill their roles.

As it is clear from the tweets, mothers who tweeted about these
failures of maternal devotion did so even when there were compelling reasons for the failure or absence and even when another
adult—the father, for example—had completed the task or been
present for the child. Thus, it is not only what mothers do but
also what they fail to do that can a #badmom label. The tweets
in this category rarely contain the humour or the additional tags
that suggest the mothers' awareness of the expectations but not
their feeling guilty about violating them. Instead, these tweets
suggest a sincere confession of failing to meet the standards of
mothering.

Inappropriate Emotional Response to Mothering.

Although most tweets labelled with the #badmom tags relate to
behavior (of the mother, the child, or others) reflecting poorly on
the mother, some tweets focus on mothers' assessments that their
emotions did not reflect the responses that they should have to
motherhood. Mothers assessed themselves negatively when they
did not feel the way they "should" about their children.

> Whenever an adult tells me that my child is "a delight to
> have in [whatever activity]" I always feel like they've got
> the wrong kid. #badmom

> So got pics [of] son from teacher asking what is causing
> red dots on his face. My 1st reaction did he draw on his
> face. Not is he sick. #badmom

> Oh sweet heavens ... Jon has his first loose tooth. It's killing

me not because he's growing up, but because it grosses me out. #BadMommy

In these examples, the writers have a particular idea about how they, as mothers, should feel in a situation, and have assessed their own emotional response as inappropriate relative to that idea. One of the most common ways that this theme revealed itself in the tweets was maternal admission of stress.

Is it horrible that I need a Xanax to help my kids with their homework? #badmommy

Totally freaking out about having another human soon.My 3rd human.Going from man to man to zone. Dont think I can do this. #badmommy

You know you're a #badmommy when you need a glass of wine to get through a weekend alone with the kids.

Consistent with the "supermom" paradigm that reflects the ideology of intensive mothering, these mothers believe that good mothering identity should not include significant feelings of stress. Similarly, mothers also evaluated themselves negatively for not enjoying particular moments or tasks that are typically associated with mothering.

Words can't express how much I hate making school lunches. #badmom #pickyeaters

Having to be in shade because of baby is making me resentful. #badmother

Although there is a cultural understanding that mothering can be stressful and some tasks of mothering can be unpleasant, even while being rewarding, the mothers who write these tweets believe that there is a limit to the stress or annoyance they should feel and they have exceeded that appropriate level.

Although some tweets label certain emotional responses as bad, such as stress or ambivalence related to particular parenting duties, others indicate that positive emotions can also be problematic, particularly when those emotions are specifically expressions of enjoyment of time away from the children.

WOOO HOOOO! First day of school! #badmommy

All these parents crying on Facebook because their kids are going (back) to school, and I'm not fazed at all. #badmom

My teens will be back home tomorrow & I really kinda wish they weren't. It's been lovely not having them around. #badmother

To assess positive feelings of relief and enjoyment as problematic if they are focused on not engaging the mothering role is consistent with the cultural emphasis on intensive mothering. A belief that these feelings are wrong also suggests that women simply should enjoy motherhood above all else. If they do not, however, it is representative of a personal flaw rather than of issues inherent in the role and its associated demands.

In all, mothers on Twitter assessed their own maternal behaviour negatively when it seemed to harm the happiness of their children, reflected too much focus on the mother's needs or desires, indicated a lack of devotion to the obligations of motherhood, or suggested that the mother's emotional responses were not always consistent with a child-centred approach to parenting. Although the vast majority of tweets using #badmom-related hashtags were an indictment of mothers, some tweets rejected or transformed the expectations of motherhood.

REJECTION AND TRANSFORMATION

Some mothers used the #badmom tags to challenge the intensive-mothering paradigm. The tweets varied in the level of their challenge. Some writers worded tweets to suggest uncertainty about whether behaviour should be labelled as bad. Other mothers indicated they understood that a particular behavior or attitude may be negatively assessed by including the #badmom hashtags, but they used the juxtaposition of other tags or terms to show that they did not believe or care about that assessment. Finally, and more forcefully, a few mothers used the #badmom tags with an explicit purpose of challenging societal expectations regarding motherhood, via linking to blog posts addressing intensive-mothering practices through a critical lens.

In some tweets, mothers question whether their behavior was "bad" or not by turning the #badmom hashtags into questions, which suggests an ambivalence about their acceptance of the intensive-mothering ideology. This critical inquiry occurred by adding a question mark to the tag or applying both a #badmom and #goodmom label.

Sunday night already? Weekend was busy. Did not do 1 bit of laundry. #screwed #no1hasNythingtoWear #badmom?

My five year old sneaks a peek at Walking Dead. It's cool cause she says fake blood is just ketchup. #badmom #awesomemom

Through the use of question marks or juxtaposition of opposing evaluations, these mothers express ambivalence about whether a particular enactment represents bad mothering. Somewhat more forcefully, other mothers were aware particular behaviors could or would be labelled as bad mothering but refused to accept shame or guilt.

My 11 year old got a Fitbit yesterday so I'm off out to walk till I pass out. She will not beat my daily steps. #badmother #sorrynotsorry

When your kid is so exhausted they oversleep and you let them. #goodmom #badmom #dontcare #workingtoohard #girlneedshersleep

Such a sentiment is also present in tweets that include the mother's laughter or joy over the violation.

Tweets that slyly challenge the intensive mothering model by using humour or word choices are common across this data set, particularly in posts related to excessive self-focus or inappropriate emotional response. Although these posts do represent some level of rejection, or at least questioning, of the intensive-mothering paradigm, the writers do not address the larger issues related to these mothering expectations or challenge the assessment on a more comprehensive level.

Of the 533 tweets that I examined, only six, or just over 1 percent, tackle the #badmom label directly. Given the limits of Twitter as a vehicle for rhetorical argument, it is not surprising that these tweets linked to blogs in which the writer had made a more developed argument about the evaluation of mothers and maternal "perfection."

> I'm a Bad Mom! Don't Judge! ow.ly/Sgjqi #BadMom #Mom #DontJudge Support each other!

> My 4 yr old has 5 cavities—does that make me a #BADMOM? NO! onepickychick.com/2015/09/help-m. #mediabloggers

> Some days just need to end!" Being a #mom can be hard. Admitting this doesn't make you a #badmom, you're normal! bit.ly/1FQtExA

Although limited in number, the tweets in this final category represent a different use of the #badmoom hashtags; they use the tag to draw the attention of the #badmom audience, and then promote a different understanding of mothering. However, given the limitations on fully developing a rhetorical argument on Twitter, these examples all linked to longer, more developed discussions in other formats.

CONCLUSIONS

Use of #badmom-related hashtags on Twitter is not unusual. Many tweets are evaluations of others as not appropriately upholding the standards of motherhood. Those tweets, written by men and women, assign blame to famous and nonfamous mothers with children of all ages. Mothers also write tweets as an evaluation of their own behavior, which leads to the question of why mothers would publicly declaim their maternal failures. In part, this question is answered by examination of the tweets themselves.

The self-assessment tweets labelled with the #badmom tags are, by use of the tag, directed at others who would identify with that topic—presumably other mothers. It is important to note that what is occurring in these tweets is confession, not justification or apology. Confessional rhetoric is characterized by self-reflection and contains a confession of moral defects (Jasinski 101). The confession is a common rhetorical act from and directed to women (Mandziuk; Honey). It is intended to evoke the judgment of others and to pass judgment on the self, and through that act to cathartically remove feelings of guilt and become exonerated for the error (Foucault 62). However, it also provides the reader with a tool that heals, as it shows that others (women, mothers, etc.) also fail in these ways and can be redeemed.

In the past, women's confessional magazines, such as *True Story* in the early twentieth-century (Mandziuk), and television shows directed at women, such as *Maury* in the late twentieth-century, have used the confessional format to great success. Although such formats did not allow all individuals to participate in the public confession, they could vicariously be part of the experience of confession and exoneration and, thus, could experience a sensation of forgiveness for their own transgressions. Today, social media forms, such as Twitter, create more opportunity for confessing to an audience fit to judge, but are anonymous enough to avoid significant social censure for the confessor (Kantrowitz-Gordon 876-877). Social media also provides the participant with the opportunity to see the confessions of others.

It is important to note that the transgressions discussed in #badmom tweets are of low negative impact on the child, which is consistent with past findings. In her analysis of one Twitter user's stream, Zappavigna found instances of tweets using self-deprecation hashtags related to #badmom. She argues that the tags invoke a play frame, in which the "aberrant bond is jokingly dismissed" (218). Thus, mothers are able to use the tweets to admit to their mothering fallibility; however, the severity of their infractions is so minor or limited that the transgression can be absorbed or laughed at. Through that laughter or dismissal, the violation is forgiven, even as it is confessed.

By presenting their own failings to an audience of other mothers, the mothers who tweet about #badmom moments invoke and reaffirm the contemporary standards of intensive mothering. At the same time, as these mothers admit to breaking the code, they are subtly building a case for the difficulty of adhering to it, which makes such deviations more palatable within the community of mothers. Mothers using this tag to openly challenge expectations of motherhood in the date pool was rare; however, the use of the tag in admission of relatively minor but frequent failings, particularly within a frame of play or dismissal, is a sly challenge to the status quo.

The examination discussed here is limited temporally, as it represents only sixty days of tweets using the three selected hashtags. Additionally, these tags are only a portion of what I could have selected. Other tags, including #badmama and #badmami, are also potential identifiers for such discussions. Finally, not all tweets that discuss mothering "failures" or challenge the societal expectations of mothers occur with these tags.

Although this work represents a limited discussion of the (re) construction of mothering by mothers on Twitter, it suggests that the power of microblogging to impact our understandings of the maternal experience should not be overlooked. From #occupywallstreet to #blacklivesmatter, Twitter has become a force for gathering public support for social change. Moving forwards, perhaps, mothers will become more assertive when challenging mothering ideology in this communicative form.

NOTE

[1] While tweets are public artifacts, Twitter usernames have not been reproduced here, in an attempt to protect user privacy. Additionally, to fairly represent the linguistic conventions and theoretically spontaneous style of Twitter, no corrections or alterations have been made to the text of tweets, beyond the removal of emoticons

difficult to reproduce in this format, and corrections to punctuation necessary for clarity.

WORKS CITED

Arnold, Lorin B. "I Don't Know Where I End and You Begin: Challenging Boundaries of Self and Intensive Mothering." *Intensive Mothering: The Cultural Contradictions of Modern Motherhood*, edited by Linda Ennis, Demeter, 2014, pp. 47-65.

Christopher, Karen. "Extensive Mothering: Employed Mothers' Constructions of the Good Mother." *Gender & Society*, vol. 26, no.1, 2012, pp. 73-96.

"Company: About." *Twitter*. Twitter, 12 Dec.2015, www.twitter. com.

Ennis, Linda. *Intensive Mothering: The Cultural Contradictions of Modern Motherhood*. Demeter, 2014.

Foucault, Michel. *The History of Sexuality, Vol 1: An Introduction*. Vintage, 1990.

Hays, Sharon. *The Cultural Contradictions of Motherhood*. Yale University Press, 1996. Print.

Honey, Maureen. "The Confession Formula and Fantasies of Empowerment." *Women's Studies*, vol. 10, no. 3, 1984, pp. 303-320.

Johnston, Deirdre D., and Deb H. Swanson. "Constructing the 'Good Mother': The Experience of Mothering Ideologies by Work Status." *Sex Roles*, vol. 54, no. 7/8, 2006, pp. 509-519.

Kantrowitz-Gordon, Ira. "Internet Confessions of Postpartum Depression." *Issues in Mental Health Nursing* 34, no. 12, 2013, pp. 874-882.

Mandziuk, Roseann. "Confessional Discourse and Modern Desires: Power and Please in *True Story* Magazine." *Critical Studies in Mass Communication*, vol. 18, no. 2, 2011, pp. 174-193.

Marwick, Alice E., and Danah Boyd. "I Tweet Honestly, I Tweet Passionately: Twitter Users, Context Collapse, and the Imagined Audience." *New Media & Society*, vol. 13, no.1, 2011, pp. 114-133.

Thornton, Leslie-Jean. "'Time of the Month' on Twitter: Taboo, Stereotype and Bonding in a No-Holds-Barred Public Arena." *Sex Roles*, vol. 68, pp. 41-54.

Zappavigna, Michele. "Enacting Identity in Microblogging through Ambient Affiliation." *Discourse & Communication*, vol. 8, no. 2, 2014, pp. 209-228.

II.
SUPPORTING MOTHERS THROUGH
SOCIAL MEDIA

4.

Boobs, Babes, and Boots

Breastfeeding Support, Facebook, and Military Mothers

AMY BARRON SMOLINSKI

B REASTFEEDING IS REGAINING acknowledgement and recognition as the biologically normal and optimal way to
nourish and nurture children. After nearly a century of
waning popularity due to medical fascination with "scientific" and
easily quantifiable feeding methods, Western society's patriarchal
devaluation of the female body and its normal physiological processes, and aggressive and often unethical marketing of breastmilk
substitutes by multinational corporations (Kaplan and Graff; Van
Esterik), the renewed appeal of breastfeeding is indebted, in part,
to new research that demonstrates the importance breastfeeding
has on lifelong health of both breastfeeding mothers and breastfed
children (Anholm; U.S. Dept. of Health and Human Services).
Research also shows that a woman's ability to successfully meet
her own breastfeeding goals depends largely on whether she has
access to knowledgeable support; and the most effective support
is generally provided by a woman's partner and her peers (Raj and
Plichta; Bar-Yam and Darby).

For most of human history, a woman's local community provided peer support throughout her mothering journey (Riordan and
Wambach 51). Women at similar stages of mothering traditionally
came together around cooking fires, spinning circles, and laundry
to share their experiences and learn from each other. As the In-
dustrial Revolution swept Western civilization, a woman's peers
depended on her social status, which was generally determined
by her marriage (Yalom). Women utilized peer support across
all social strata—from ladies-in-waiting who attended to royal

and noblewomen during their customary lying-in after birth, to lower-class women's workplace talk on factory assembly lines or in the marketplace.

Towards the end of the twentieth century, people became more mobile. It is no longer the norm, especially in the United States, for people to remain in one place their entire lives. No longer do most women have the assurance of childhood friends, female relatives, or even their husband's female relatives to rely on for guidance in mothering. As society becomes more mobile and transient, mothers struggle to find one other, and they invent and embrace new ways of seeking out other women's experience and wisdom. Often, this highly mobile and transient lifestyle leads to deep feelings of isolation, uncertainty, and depression and anxiety, especially in new or first-time mothers (Robertson et al).

To cope with this sense of isolation, Generation Y and millennial mothers use mobile technology to recreate their village, or the support networks traditionally found in personal connections with friend, neighbours, and relatives. As digital natives, today's mothers are innately comfortable with using mobile technology in the form of smartphones and tablets, and the wide variety of social media platforms available through these devices. In a critical ethnographic study of African American mothers in the U.S., Ifeyinwa Asiodu and her colleagues found that "Regardless of educational background, income, or living situation, each participant had a smartphone ... or access to one" (Asiodu et al). This sample may be extrapolated to the greater American population, 90 percent of whom have a smartphone (Duggan and Smith).

In addition to the psychosocial support provided by online communities, healthcare professionals are exploring ways to leverage mobile technology to support health promotion and disease prevention. In 2011, the World Health Organization (WHO) termed this phenomenon "mobile health" and defined it as "medical and public health practice supported by mobile devices" (WHO). Mobile health platforms have been extremely successful in promoting public health issues by reaching individuals on a regular basis in their day-to-day lives, right at their fingertips. The Text4Baby program sends targeted perinatal health messages on a regular basis to pregnant and new mothers (Evans et al). Former Surgeon General of the Army Patricia Horoho created an Army-wide initiative in 2012 aimed at reaching military healthcare beneficiaries in what she termed "the white spaces of their lives," meaning the times and places outside of encounters with healthcare providers, when people make daily decisions impacting their health. She advocated the use of mobile health to track and support lifestyle choices that promote health and wellness (Horoho).

In the field of lactation support, it has been a growing trend that breastfeeding parents seeking help prefer to communicate with lactation professionals via text, chat, or private message, and often over social media platforms (Bickford). The International Board of Lactation Consultant Examiners, or IBLCE, has issued strongly worded guidance against utilizing social media platforms to communicate with clients, citing fears about client confidentiality (IBLCE). However, most lactation professionals find that millennial clients are not willing to reach out for help in person or even via telephone calls. Within the evolving field of professional lactation support, there is ongoing debate about how to strike the right balance on social media. Lactation professionals need to reach millennial mothers in the milieu in which they are most comfortable, yet maintain professional bearing and provide education and accurate, evidence-based breastfeeding information in ways that are accessible to the demographic of contemporary parents (Brooks; Bickford; McCann and McCulloch).

In this chapter, I discuss one of the most highly mobile, transient, and segregated populations within the United States: the U.S. Military Forces and their families. Military families make up one percent of the U.S. population (Segal and Segal), and their lives are structured according to the needs of the military. For the purposes of this chapter, and to reflect the realities of the twenty-first century U.S. Military, it is important to understand that any reference to "military families" encompasses a diverse and changing demographic. Although most military families still follow the traditional demographic of a male servicemember spouse and a female civilian spouse, there are also female servicemembers married to civilian males, dual-military spouses, single-parent families, and same-sex spouses, in which one or both partners may serve on active duty. Accordingly, "military mothers" refers to both mothers who are married to military servicemembers and active duty servicemembers who are mothers.

Within military culture, the topics of breastfeeding and social media are both hot-button issues, which frequently intertwine. In recent years, massive controversies surrounding breastfeeding and the military have played out on social media, often with little follow-up reporting on the end results (Peterson Beadle; Basu). A more nuanced, in-depth analysis of the realities of breastfeeding within military culture reveals its complex and, sometimes, tense relationship with social media. As executive director of Mom2Mom Global, a nonprofit organization dedicated to supporting breastfeeding military families, and in my previous positions within the organization, I have observed this relationship for nearly a decade.

I joined Mom2Mom's first chapter, Mom2Mom KMC, in 2008 as a Peer Mentor. In 2010, I became the first community outreach director, and I helped create the first board of directors dedicated to growing the organization into a sustainable, thriving peer support network. From 2010 on, social media has been an integral piece of our operations in carrying out our mission. In 2015, I accepted the task of founding Mom2Mom Global to expand our mission and reach to families in military communities worldwide. We use social media on a daily basis to promote, protect, and support breastfeeding military families. As a geographically diverse governing board, we also use numerous virtual networking and social platforms to communicate and carry out our organizational operations. I am also the spouse of an active duty servicemember and the mother of four children, all of whom I have breastfed. Through my work with Mom2Mom as both a leader and a participant, I have been at the crossroads where military culture, breastfeeding, and social media intersect for nearly as long as I have been a mother.

Breastfeeding is highly recommended by military medical practitioners. Most military families receive their health care at military treatment facilities (MTFs), where they have access to free medical care. Regular health screenings and strict medical requirements (for example, no one with HIV is allowed to serve on active duty), coupled with free prenatal care, means that military families are a remarkably healthy population subset and that most pregnancies are low risk. High-risk prenatal factors are identified early and monitored carefully. Additionally, prenatal education is free, easily accessible, and available through a multitude of resources, and nearly all prenatal classes include at least an introductory discussion of breastfeeding. A handful of MTFs are accredited Baby-Friendly Hospitals, and many others have identified lactation support as a key quality measure for emphasis, even creating official breastfeeding policies to support both patients and employees who breastfeed. The American College of Obstetricians and Gynecologists, the American Association of Pediatricians, and most other professional medical associations recommend exclusive breastfeeding for the first six months of life, so pregnant patients are routinely advised by providers and staff to breastfeed. Of course, as a microcosm of the U.S. population and culture, military medicine also reflects many of the common pitfalls that undermine breastfeeding in civilian hospitals. Lack of consistent, updated staff training, inadequate access to trained lactation professionals, and health care provider bias based on personal experience often lead to mothers' confusion, physical discomfort, and uncertainty about breastfeeding (Losch; Dillaway; Ramakrishnan et al.).

This confusion is compounded by the realities of the military lifestyle. On average, military families move every two to three years (United States GAO). Often, this means that a woman may be relocated either during pregnancy or just a few weeks after having a baby. In cases of overseas moves, this frequently means that a family's belongings are en route to a new duty station, and, sometimes, the baby is brought home from the hospital to temporary lodging. Moves are commonly over great geographic distance, which separates a new mother from her trusted support network of family and friends. Although some military families are fortunate to have extended family willing to travel to help with a new baby, the cost and distance are often prohibitive. For many families, especially those stationed overseas, multiple time zones also complicate communication attempts with family and friends who may wish to offer support. Even when a baby is born to a geographically stable military family, a new mother's spouse is frequently not physically present. Frequent deployments, extended temporary duty assignments, and long shift hours for the military servicemember may leave a mother caring for her new baby and any older children as a virtually single parent.

In the face of these challenges, military families have proven remarkably adept in the practice of one of the U.S. Army's mottoes: "adapt and overcome." Successful military families learn how to reach out for assistance and support in new duty stations. In addition to traditional means of networking, such as church and school groups and spouses clubs or service organizations, social media has become a vital part of military family networking in the twenty-first century (Sherman et al). Facebook, in particular, has become one of the most valuable tools in a military mother's repertoire. In nearly every military community around the world, there are Facebook groups specific to the unique needs and interests of military families. This is particularly true for parenting support groups, which are usually thematically categorized into homeschooling groups, pregnancy and childbirth groups, infant and toddler groups, twin parent groups, and natural or attachment parenting groups. Breastfeeding support groups, in particular, have become a lifeline for military mothers seeking assistance, reassurance, and validation throughout their breastfeeding journey.

Mom2Mom Global is a network of breastfeeding peer support groups specific to military communities; they are rapidly expanding to fill the needs of breastfeeding military families. Founded in Germany in 1999 by a neonatologist, his wife (a breastfeeding mother), a maternal-child nurse and a pediatrician, the group began as Mom2Mom in the Kaiserslautern Military Community (KMC), which is home to Landstuhl Regional Medical Center, Ramstein Air Base, and a handful of other small military installations that comprise the largest American population outside of U.S. borders. Originally founded at Landstuhl Regional Medical Center, Mom2Mom KMC was created to partner pregnant and breastfeeding mothers with Peer Mentors, and this continues to be the signature support program in today's Mom2Mom Global chapters (Barron Smolinski and Heald). To qualify as a Mom2Mom Peer Mentor, a mother must have breastfed a minimum of six months and have considered it a positive experience. Eligible military mothers take a free one-day training session taught by Mom2Mom chapter leadership at their local military installation. Although the Peer

Mentorship program remains the hallmark of modern Mom2Mom chapters, the program has expanded over time to include regularly scheduled group meetings and support for lactation education and training in military communities. Mom2Mom Global chapters have embraced social media, particularly Facebook, as an easy and effective way for military mothers to access breastfeeding support twenty-four hours a day (Barron Smolinski and Heald).

In contemporary military life, Facebook is one of the first places a family will turn for information when they receive new orders. Many pregnant or breastfeeding mothers seek out online breast-feeding support in their new military communities before they even leave their current homes. As Mom2Mom KMC members moved on to new duty stations, they often reported frustration and sadness at the lack of peer support they found. A significant number requested to stay in the Mom2Mom KMC Facebook group to continue to receive support and accurate information as they continued their breastfeeding journeys. Many mothers continued to breastfeed past the culturally accepted norms of infancy, and the Facebook group supported them through new challenges of breastfeeding toddlers and/or continuing to tandem-breastfeed through a subsequent pregnancy and with a new baby. Often, for-mer members requested to add their friends or family members to the group, or they sought to connect them with one of the trained lactation professionals they had known through Mom2Mom KMC. Lactation professionals in Germany frequently found themselves seeking colleagues and resources in U.S. locations for breastfeeding mothers who needed professional support near to them. As the Mom2Mom KMC legacy grew so too did the reach of its trained lactation professionals and Peer Mentors.

When the original four founders created Mom2Mom in 1999, they envisioned that it would be replicated at other military in-stallations to fulfill the need for military-specific breastfeeding peer support (Barron Smolinski and Heald). In what is perhaps a logical progression, former members of Mom2Mom KMC, many of whom had trained to become both Peer Mentors and Certified Lactation Counselors during their tenure in Germany, began to create new Mom2Mom chapters in other military communities. Both breastfeeding and peer counselling are learned skill sets that integrate into a woman's heuristic perspective and honour her intuitive knowledge. Once that knowledge is woven into a woman's sense of self, she does not leave those skills behind when she travels to make a life in a new place, as almost all military spouses do. A woman who has integrated a sense of value of her experience and skills leverages those skills as a way to connect with other mothers by offering them the kind of support from which she and her children benefitted.

By 2015, Mom2Mom KMC had grown to an immense organization locally, and the five-member board of directors was unable to provide adequate support for new chapters while still fulfilling its duty to operate the KMC organization. In June 2015, Mom2Mom KMC voted to create a separate organization, Mom2Mom Global, to oversee the creation and operation of all Mom2Mom chapters throughout the military, and I accepted the position of executive director of this newly formed organization. One of the largest responsibilities of Mom2Mom Global has been the development and implementation of social media policies and strategies to fulfill its mission of accurate, inclusive breastfeeding support for all military mothers.

The importance of social media in today's breastfeeding support networks cannot be overstated. Research shows that most millennial mothers first seek out parenting and medical advice from online forums, such as Facebook groups (Ray). Mother-to-mother support is still vitally important in face-to-face contexts, but the realities of geographic location, transportation, and employment status have made it exceedingly difficult for many modern parents to benefit from this kind of close contact. Humans are social creatures, and we have developed technological means to meet our need for social interaction, validation, and support. This is true of any breastfeeding family in the twenty-first century, but for military families, social media is often the difference between a mother meeting her breastfeeding goal or prematurely weaning (Audelo).

Mom2Mom Global chapters operate closed Facebook groups administered by accredited lactation professionals. In each military community, these groups offer a safe place for mothers to ask questions, voice concerns, solicit peer support, vent frustrations, celebrate milestones, and share breastfeeding images. Carefully developed policies are strictly enforced to ensure members' confidentiality and the security of the groups. Mom2Mom Global's comments policy requires all comments and discussions to be phrased in a respectful and nonjudgmental way that supports and respects each woman's individual breastfeeding goal. Anyone who violates these policies is immediately removed from the group.

Breastfeeding is something of a lost art that is currently regaining acceptance as a culturally acceptable behaviour, and like all women's health issues, it is fraught with myths, half-truths, and inaccuracies that reflect cultural and personal biases. Trained lactation professionals provide breastfeeding education and live links to cite evidence-based research in group discussions. Topics discussed in conversation threads then become searchable within the group for later reference when other mothers have similar questions. In this way, accurate information is integrated into the peer advice given from mother to mother. For women with acute or severe concerns requiring individual professional lactation counselling or medical advice, these closed Facebook groups can act as a triage. Whereas generation Y mothers depended on "Dr. Google" to answer their questions, millennial mothers tend to rely on the consensus of social media contacts (Ray). Closed groups dedicated to the dissemination of accurate information provide an initial screening, which ensures that these mothers and their children will not slip through the cracks in the event that they require specialized care.

Breastfeeding is a mothering practice that requires visual learning and reinforcement, round-the-clock support, and a strong peer network to ensure optimal success (Kendall-Tackett). Social media communities provide all of these elements for today's breastfeeding mothers. Photo and video sharing capabilities mean that women can easily see images of other mothers breastfeeding their children. This normalizes a mother's experience, provides her with a point of reference for self-directed learning, and assuages feelings of doubt, isolation, and fear that she may have about breastfeeding. Breastfeeding is a "right-brained" activity, meaning it must be seen to be learned (Kendall-Tackett). In many cases, modern mothers come from families in which breastfeeding has not been practised for two generations. Mothers who have never seen a human baby breastfeed are often overwhelmed by the fear that they are "doing it wrong." Visual media of breastfeeding dyads reassure mothers that they and their babies are "normal." They also offer mothers visual suggestions for positioning, latching techniques, and sensory experiences, such as the physical and emotional feelings common to breastfeeding, which they may never have otherwise considered.

One example of a visually learned technique is biological nurturing, or the "laid-back breastfeeding" position (Colson et al.; Mohrbacher). The cultural norm of infant feeding has been established through images of babies feeding in a supine position, facing up towards the ceiling with their bodies turned away from the caregiver, with a bottle placed in the baby's mouth. Breastfeeding mothers typically mimic a modified version of this bottle-feeding position using a "cradle" or "cross-cradle" hold to bring the baby to the breast in a near-supine position. Research into biological nurturing found that a more biologically and physiologically effective position is actually for the mother to semi-recline, with baby prone on top of her, which allows the baby to self-attach to the breast (Colson et al). This position encourages the baby to use all of his or her muscles and work with gravity to latch onto the breast, and often benefits the mother by providing a deeper, more comfortable latch. For a mother who has never seen a baby feed in anything other than the supine bottle-feeding position, the idea of leaning back and placing her baby on top of her chest sounds preposterous. But when that same mother sees a photo or video of another mother and baby using the laid-back position, it becomes a possibility that she is willing to try.

Mom2Mom chapters operate closed, private Facebook groups that function as twenty-four-hour breastfeeding support groups. At any time of the day or night, when a mother is up nursing her baby and checks social media, she is almost guaranteed to find another mother breastfeeding her baby. A mother who needs help with a breastfeeding concern, or simply desires support and reassurance that it is normal for her baby to be waking frequently to feed, will find it in these groups. Women who are experiencing negative feedback about breastfeeding within their community or close circle of family and friends feel safe sharing their experiences inside a closed confidential online group. Many times, the other mothers in the group can offer suggestions for coping with or overcoming this resistance. A mother, who may be fearful of posting breastfeeding visual media on her personal social media accounts, often feels safe sharing these photos or videos within a closed group—where she knows these images will be received positively and she will be celebrated for overcoming obstacles or meeting the breastfeeding milestones or goals she has set for herself and her baby. Women who have babies of similar ages often bond over shared experiences and stages, and online friendships often develop into in-person friendships when women meet with their children through support groups or privately with one another.

Mom2Mom Facebook groups have become catalysts for community change in unexpected ways. Trends have emerged within each local community regarding where breastfeeding families find support or obstacles in public places, health care facilities, and military family support organizations. Rather than suffer in isolation, mothers who face challenges or negativity are networking in the spirit of advocacy, which leads to action, through appropriate formal feedback channels or chains of command, and positive social change. For example, mothers within these safe, confidential groups commonly share information about which medical practitioners provide knowledgeable and supportive breastfeeding care and which providers consistently give outdated advice based on personal bias. If one mother details a negative experience breastfeeding in public on a military installation, it is common for other mothers to have similar problems. Under federal law, it is illegal for anyone to interfere with a breastfeeding mother and child anywhere on federal property, as long as they are authorized to be there (U.S. Congress). Therefore, when illegal and ill-informed actions against breastfeeding are brought to light, mothers feel empowered to utilize the formal channels within the military to file complaints and demand better training and education of installation personnel to ensure compliance with federal law. Mothers who use these channels have reported to me a sense of both personal empowerment and deep satisfaction that their actions are able to improve conditions for future breastfeeding mothers and their children.

Military servicemembers, health care providers, and other community members who join the groups seeking breastfeeding support gain insight into why breastfeeding is important and beneficial for not only children but also for communities as a public health measure (U.S. Dept. of Health and Human Services). Additionally, they learn how to provide support to create a breastfeeding-friendly culture in both virtual and real world environments and how to increase breastfeeding initiation and duration rates, which supports the public health of military families. An active duty dentist joined her local Mom2Mom chapter's Facebook group when she gave birth to her own child, who was born with *ankyloglossia*, or tongue-tie, a relatively common but poorly understood oral anatomical anomaly that can have a devastating impact on breastfeeding. After overcoming her personal struggles with the help of her local Mom2Mom peer support, she trained to become a Certified Lactation Counselor and sought mentorship from a pediatric dentist who specializes in treatment of infant *ankyloglossia*. She now routinely performs *ankyloglossia* releases on breastfeeding babies in the community.

In addition to creating a personal and local village, online breastfeeding support groups create a global village. Mom2Mom Global and several of its local chapters also operate public social media profiles. Facebook pages, Instagram, Twitter, and Pinterest accounts all provide ways to interact with the public and with other breastfeeding advocacy groups. Through these public profiles, members of Mom2Mom can find other resources, such as leading lactation professionals' blogs, as well as information regarding political and cultural group actions to raise awareness about breastfeeding, which inevitably informs and strengthens their experience of breastfeeding. In particular, Mom2Mom Global has formed a strong alliance with Breastfeeding in Combat Boots—a website, blog, and social media presence founded by Robyn Roche-Paull. A former Navy corpsman, Roche-Paull wrote a book with the same name as her website, dedicated to supporting and empowering active duty military mothers who breastfeed (Roche-Paull). This partnership has been built exclusively through social media contact. Together, our organizations strive to bring breastfeeding concerns from the families who face the daily struggles to the highest levels of Department of Defense (DoD) policy and procedural authorities. Through public social media, the military has seen vast forward momentum in the support, promotion, and protection of breastfeeding as a public health issue. A significant step forward in DoD acceptance and support of breastfeeding is their recent memorandum expanding paid maternity leave to twelve weeks and mandating a designated lactation space in all units with more than fifty women (Carter).

Social media has played an influential role in bringing breastfeeding to the forefront of DoD consideration. In 2015, a photograph of soldiers breastfeeding in uniform that was taken to decorate the lactation room at Ft. Bliss, TX, also resulted in controversy when the photo went viral on social media (Basu). This was not the first incident in which breastfeeding, social media, and the military resulted in controversy.

This photo of Air Force Sgt. Terran Echegoyen McCabe, left, and Staff Sgt. Christina Luna breastfeeding initially was considered controversial but eventually resulted in the Air Force clarifying its policy to explicitly permit breastfeeding in uniform, so long as "professional decorum" is preserved. Photo credit: Brynja Sigurdottir Photography

In 2012, two Airmen posed for a breastfeeding photo in uniform (Peterson Beadle). They had secured permission from their chain of command and public affairs office to do so as part of an awareness-raising campaign for World Breastfeeding Week. The photo went viral and remained a controversial headline news item for months because it featured two active duty personnel breastfeeding in uniform. What was not reported was the Air Force's final response to that story. They modified their official regulation to explicitly permit breastfeeding in uniform (AFI 44-102). More recently, commanders at military installations in Hawaii and Idaho attempted to pass policies restricting breastfeeding on their installations (Martin-Weber; Roche-Paull; Rowland). Not only were these attempts poor public health policy, but they were also in violation of federal law and existing DoD regulations for each service branch. In both cases, the public outcry from social media resulted in the policies being rescinded (Martin-Weber; Roche-Paull; Rowland). Breastfeeding military families are exceptionally skilled at adapting to ever-changing family situations. Perhaps more so than many others, military mothers are also remarkably adept at "working the system." The military is a closed system. It is laborious and often circuitous, but like all closed systems, once one figures out how it functions, anyone can be a powerful agent for positive change for all. Military mothers understand this innately because our entire lives take place within the military system. Social media has become an invaluable tool for military mothers to create and maintain healthy families and responsive communities as well as to promote worldwide cultural change. For many of these mothers the ability to meet their breastfeeding goals has been enabled by social media, which has facilitated unprecedented personal, cultural, and generational empowerment. It is my privilege to observe and participate in the mothering journeys of these remarkable women, and social media is the web that keeps us connected.

WORKS CITED

American Public Health Association (APHA). *Breastfeeding and Social Media*, APHA, 2015. www.apha.org/news-and-media/news-releases/apha-news-releases/breastfeeding-and-social-media. Accessed 25 July 2016.

Anholm, Cheryl Hancock. "Breastfeeding: A Preventive Approach to Health Care in Infancy." *Issues in Comprehensive Pediatric Nursing*, vol. 9, no. 1, 1986, pp. 1-10.

Audelo, Lara. "Connecting with Today's Mothers: Breastfeeding Support Online." *Clinical Lactation*, vol. 5, no. 1, 2014, pp. 16-19.

Asiodu, Ifeyinwa V. et al. "Breastfeeding and Use of Social Media Among First-Time African American Mothers." *Journal of Obstetric, Gynecologic & Neonatal Nursing*, 44.2 (2015): 268-278. Web.

Barron Smolinski, Amy, and Tamra Heald. "Mom2Mom KMC: From Peer Mentoring to Community Change." GOLD Lactation Online Conference 2015. 5 May 2015, Lecture, www.goldlactation.com. Accessed 24 Aug. 2016.

Bar-Yam, Naomi Bromberg, and Lori Darby. "Fathers and Breastfeeding: A Review of the Literature." *Journal of Human Lactation*, vol. 13, no. 1, 1997, pp. 45-50.

Basu, Tanya. "Photo of Soldiers Breastfeeding Goes Viral." *Time*, Time Inc., 13 Sept. 2015, www.time.com/4032913/female-soldiers-breastfeeding/. Accessed 13 Dec. 2015.

Bickford, Fleur. "Breastfeeding and Social Media Video." *Ameda*. Ameda, www.ameda.com/healthcare-professionals/professional-webinars/bickford-webinar-video. Accessed 25 July 2016.

Brooks, Elizabeth C. "What's Too 'Friendly' For an IBCLC on Social Media?" GOLD Lactation Online Conference 2015, 31 Aug. 2015, Lecture, www.goldlactation.com. Accessed 24 Aug. 2016.

Carter, Ash. *DoD-Wide Changes to Maternity Leave*. U.S. Department of Defense, 2015, http://breastfeedingincombatboots.com/wp-content/uploads/2016/02/OSD001197-16-FOD-FINAL.pdf. Accessed 25 Feb. 2016.

Colson, S. D. et al. "Optimal Positions Triggering Primitive Neonatal Reflexes Stimulating Breastfeeding." *Early Human Development*, vol. 84, no. 7, 2008, pp. 441-449. *Pub Med*, doi: 0.1016/j.earlhumdev. 2007.12.003.

Dillaway, H. E. "Are Pediatric Offices "Supportive" of Breastfeeding? Discrepancies between Mothers' and Healthcare Professionals' Reports." *Clinical Pediatrics*, vol. 43, no. 5, 2004, pp. 417-430.

Duggan, M., and A. Smith. "Social Media Update 2013." *Pew Research Center*, Pew Research Center, 2014, www.pewinternet.org/files/2013/12/PIP_Social-Networking-2013.pdf. Accessed 24 Aug. 2016. Evans, W. D., et al. "Mobile Health Evaluation Methods: The Text4baby Case Study." *Journal of Health Communication*, vol. 17, sup.1, 2012, pp. 22-29. *Taylor & Francis*, doi: 10.1080/10810730.2011.649157

Horoho, Patricia D. "Plenary Remarks." 2012 Military Health System Conference, Baltimore. 31 Jan. 2012. Lecture.

International Board of Lactation Consultant Examiners (IBLCE). *Advisory Opinion: Professionalism in the Social Media Age.* IBLCE, 2015, http://iblce.org/wp-content/uploads/2015/12/Advisory-Opinion-Social-Media-Professionalism.pdf. Accessed 25 July 2016.

Kaplan, Deborah L., and Kristina M. Graff. "Marketing Breastfeeding—Reversing Corporate Influence on Infant Feeding Practices." *Journal of Urban Health*, vol. 85, no. 4, 2008, pp. 486-504.

Kendall-Tackett, Kathleen. "How Too Much Information May Cause Problems for Breastfeeding New Mothers." *Science and Sensibility*, Lamaze International, 8 Sept. 2009, www.scienceandsensibility.org/blog/how-too-much-information-may-cause-problems-for-breastfeeding-new-mothers. Accessed 13 Dec. 2015.

Losch, Mary, et al. "Impact of Attitudes on Maternal Decisions Regarding Infant Feeding." *The Journal of Pediatrics*, vol. 126, no. 4, 1995, pp. 507-514.

Martin-Weber, Jessica. "Breastfeeding Discrimination and Mountain Home Air Force Base- Interview with Breastfeeding In Combat Boots." *Theleakyboob*, The Leaky B@@b, 23 Apr. 2015, http://theleakyboob.com/2015/04/breastfeeding-discrimination-and-mountain-home-air-force-base-interview-with-breastfeeding-in-combat-boots/. Accessed 13 Dec. 2015.

McCann, A. D., and J. E. McCulloch. "Establishing an Online and Social Media Presence for Your IBCLC Practice." *Journal of Human Lactation*, vol. 28, no. 4, 2012, pp. 450-454. *Pub Med*, doi: 10.1177/0890334412461304

Mohrbacher, Nancy. "Introducing Natural Breastfeeding." *Nancy Mohrbacher.* Breastfeeding Reporter Blog, 23 Mar. 2015, www.nancymohrbacher.com/articles/2015/3/23/introducing-natural-breastfeeding.html. Accessed 13 Dec. 2015.

Peterson Beadle, Amanda. "Controversy Erupts Over Photos of Military Women Breastfeeding." *Think Progress.* Center for American Progress Action Fund, 1 June 2012, https://thinkprogress.org/controversy-erupts-over-photos-of-military-women-breastfeeding-2f967eedef2c#.fkj6jy4wo. Accessed 13 Dec. 2015.

Raj, Vinitha Krishna, and Stacey B. Plichta. "The Role of Social Support in Breastfeeding Promotion: A Literature Review." *Journal of Human Lactation*, vol. 14, no. 1, 1998, pp. 41-45.

Ramakrishnan, Rema, et al. "The Association Between Maternal Perception of Obstetric and Pediatric Care Providers' Attitudes and Exclusive Breastfeeding Outcomes." *Journal of Human Lactation*, vol. 30, no. 1, 2014, pp. 80-87.

Ray, Julie A. "Family Connections: Today's Young Families: Successful Strategies for Engaging Millennial Parents." *Childhood Education*, vol. 89, no. 5, 2013, pp. 332-334.

Riordan, Jan, and Karen Wambach. *Breastfeeding and Human Lactation*. Jones & Bartlett Learning, 2010.

Robertson, Emma, et al. "Antenatal Risk Factors for Postpartum Depression: A Synthesis of Recent Literature." *General Hospital Psychiatry*, vol. 26, no. 4, 2004, pp. 289-295.

Roche-Paull, Robyn. *Breastfeeding in Combat Boots*. Hale Publishing, 2015.

Rowland, Ashley. "Military Bases Struggle with Breast-Feeding Policies." *Stripes*, 18 June 2015, www.stripes.com/news/pacific/military-bases-struggle-with-breast-feeding-policies-1.352989. Accessed 14 Dec. 2015.

Segal, David R., and Mady Wechsler Segal. "America's Military Population." *Population Bulletin*, vol. 59, no 4, Population Reference Bureau, 2004.

Sherman, Michelle D., et al. *Social Media Communication with Military Spouses*. REACH Outreach, The University of Minnesota, 2015.

United States Air Force. *AFI 44-102*. *Static E-Publishing*, U.S. Air Force, 2015, http://static.e-publishing.af.mil/production/1/af_sg/publication/afi44-102/afi44-102.pdf. Accessed 25 Feb. 2016.

United States. United States Department of Health and Human Services. *The Surgeon General's Call to Action to Support Breastfeeding*. NCBI, 2011, www.ncbi.nlm.nih.gov/books/NBK52682/. Accessed 24 Aug. 2016.

United States. General Accounting Office. *Military Personnel: Longer Time between Moves Related to Higher Satisfaction and Retention : Briefing Report to the Chairman and Ranking Minority Member, Subcommittee on Defense, Committee on*

Appropriations, U.S. Senate. Washington: U.S. General Accounting Office, 2001.

U.S. Congress. House of Representatives. *H.R.5016 - Financial Services and General Government Appropriations Act, 2015. Congress.Gov*, Government of the United States, 2015, www.congress.gov/bill/113th-congress/house-bill/5016. 13 Dec. 2015.

Van Esterik, Penny. "The Politics of Breastfeeding." *Food and Culture: A Reader*, edited by Carole Counihan and Penny Van Esterik, Routledge, 1997, pp. 370-82. Print.

World Health Organization (WHO). *Mhealth: Second Global Survey on Ehealth. World Health Organization*, WHO, www.who.int/goe/publications/goe_mhealth_web.pdf. Accessed 24 Aug. 2016.

Yalom, Marilyn. *A History of the Wife*. HarperCollins, 2001.

5.
Mothering in the Digital Diaspora

LEAH WILLIAMS VEAZEY

MIGRANT MOTHERS FACE MULTIPLE disruptions to their social networks and identity during both the migration process and transition to motherhood, which often leads to a lack of social support at times of high need (Barclay and Kent; Rogan et al.; Benza and Liamputtong). Social media communication presents an opportunity to respond to these challenges. This chapter explores two social media strategies used by migrant mothers to create peer-support networks: closed, local diasporic online mothers' communities, such as Facebook groups, and globally dispersed open networks established through linked blogs, Twitter chats, forums, and rotating photo-sharing accounts.

This chapter uses "migrant mother" as an umbrella term to denote a mother of non-adult children who is living away from the country of her birth or upbringing. The category includes mothers in very different situations and may include refugee and asylum-seeking mothers, voluntary migrant mothers of various socioeconomic status, and expatriate mothers. They may be transnationally "mothering at a distance" (Madianou) or co-located with their children (or a combination of both). Their migration may be of a temporary nature, or aiming for settlement, may be authorized or undocumented, and may take place in a context of privilege or disadvantage. Mothers across these categories face challenges, including isolation and lack of support networks as well as conflicting cultural expectations of "good mothers" and unfamiliar, often prejudiced, health and social care systems. Despite these commonalities, a focus on social media strategies does

81

imply a focus on those migrant mothers who have access to the necessary technological apparatus and services, which may exclude newly arrived migrant mothers, mothers currently on the move, or mothers in refugee camps or detention centres.

Recommendations from research in this area often focus on encouraging health or social services to create or improve social-support networks for migrant mothers to address some of these challenges (Benza and Liamputtong; Hoang et al.; Ward; Su and Hynie). By contrast, this chapter explores how mothers have taken the initiative in this area and how they have become agents of social change rather than passive victims of systemic failure through their creation and curation of peer-support networks using social media tools. Focusing on the resourcefulness and creative endeavours of the migrant mothers in supporting their own and one another's "survival and wellness" (DeSouza, "Transforming Possibilities of Care" 88), this chapter addresses the need for "alternative discourses of migrant mothering" that highlight mothers' strengths and abilities. The chapter places their challenges in a social context, rather than repeating a "deficit discourse" (88-89), and extends this discourse into the area of networked sociality online. Through the exploration of distinct practices in which migrant mothers are engaged, this chapter highlights the commonalities and differences in the role of open and closed social media systems in creating online communities of mothers.

MOTHERING AWAY FROM HOME

Women face specific challenges when they become mothers and raise children in countries other than the ones where they were themselves raised. These may include limited instrumental and emotional support in the immediate postnatal period and beyond; idealized images of motherhood that are racially and culturally unattainable for them; and unfamiliar healthcare systems and birthing practices that may conflict with best practice "at home." If they are from cultures in which women are valued and supported in pregnancy and early motherhood, they may feel this lack in a society that does not routinely provide this support (Barclay and

Kent 4). Sandra Benza and Pranee Liamputtong's 2014 metasynthesis of fifteen studies relating to migrant mothers' experiences found that isolation and lack of support in the postpartum period were common and detrimental to the mental health of both new and experienced mothers (2).

Ruth DeSouza notes that although both migrant and nonmigrant women experience disturbances in their social networks during their transition to motherhood, establishing new support networks is arguably more difficult for migrant women who are also separated from established networks by long distances and time zones. They may also experience language difficulties in their efforts to establish new support networks through antenatal classes, mothers' groups, and playgroups. Ultimately, the lack of social support networks can lead to feelings of isolation and emotional distress as well as difficulties resulting from a lack of information and practical support (DeSouza, *New Spaces and Possibilities*).

Mothers adopt various strategies to meet the challenges presented by mothering in a new country, including proactively seeking information, establishing new peer networks, and using these networks to find appropriate care and to reclaim rituals relating to culturally specific maternal practices (DeSouza "Transforming Possibilities of Care: Goan Migrant Motherhood in New Zealand"). Namita Manohar and Erika Busse-Cárdenas argue that some migration-affected mothers deploy particular mothering strategies to respond to the difficulties posed by migration: "motherhood becomes a resource for responding to the specific structural challenges encountered in migration" (189).

CONNECTED MIGRANTS

Research indicates that social media and digital technologies have altered migrants' relationships, networks, and identities in two major areas. First, the ease and speed of communication has increased migrants' ability to maintain relationships with family and friends (Diminescu, "The Connected Migrant"). Second, social media has enabled the creation of "digital diasporas" linking globally dispersed people with a sense of a common origin (Bernal; Brinkerhoff; Diminescu, "Introduction").

This chapter uses the term "diaspora" to capture the dynamic processes of migration and belonging, dispersal and connection, which work to create "a sense of togetherness, even under the condition of geographical dispersion" (Greschke 131). A diaspora is both a network of migrants and a community formed through migration, and there is therefore, as Victoria Bernal argues, "a particular synergy between the internet's ability to form linkages among dispersed users and the relations of displacement and connection that constitutes diaspora" (Bernal 58).

Despite these developments, some migrant mothers find that connections to family and premigration friendship networks are absent or insufficient, particularly as a result of the impact of time zones or divergent lived experiences (Ryan et al. 211). Additionally, generic diaspora networks may not provide the specific support that they need as mothers. In an effort to fill these gaps, they have created mothering-specific online diaspora groups and networks.

DIGITAL MOTHERS

Studies of "digital mothers" (Gibson and Hanson) have shown the significance of social media and online communities for mothers (Moravec; Arnold; Madge and O'Connor; Wang). Mothers use social media to connect with other mothers and to communicate with existing networks of family and friends. They use it to perform their new social role as mothers (Kim et al.) and to "draw family and friends closer to them" in a "social nesting pattern" (Bartholomew et al. 464). In connecting with other mothers, they seek to increase their social capital in the form of emotional support, information giving and community protection (Drentea and Moren-Cross 939); to increase their confidence by accessing advice and sharing experiences (Gibson and Hanson); to reduce social isolation (Dunham et al.); and even to access offline support (Dunham et al.).

The potential of online mothering networks to simultaneously resist and reinforce unequal gender ideologies has also been a rich line of enquiry (Arnold; Drentea and Moren-Cross; Madge and O'Connor; Jensen). Online networks are spaces where women can perform empowered motherhood and demonstrate maternal agency (O' Reilly) but may also reinscribe restrictive and unequal gender, class, race, and heteronormative discourses. Similarly, blogging by mothers has been claimed to be a radical act (Friedman and Calixte; Lopez) by which mothers have claimed public space, voiced the complex and varied realities of motherhood, and, specifically, created discursive and supportive communities of mothers: "What many have come to understand as the most radical potential of these [mommy] blogs is their ability to foster a community among mothers that previously did not exist, one without geographical or relational boundaries" (Borda 129). However, mothers' blogs have been subject to the same criticisms as mothers' online communities. Such critiques include concern that both mother blogging and maintaining online mothering networks are practices that encourage women to expend significant emotional and creative labour on mothering in a way that is not expected of fathers.

CREATING COMMUNITIES OF MIGRANT MOTHERS ONLINE

In this chapter, I explore two distinct practices used to create community among mothers who are "away from home." The first involves locally focused, closed Facebook groups for mothers with a common ethnicity, nationality, or language. Grounded in their locality and operating within a "closed group system"—that is, participants must be both members of Facebook and approved to join a group by the group's administrators—these enclaved mothers' groups create communities where mothers can find people "like themselves" in their local area, for example Thai mothers in Sydney or French mothers in Hong Kong.

In contrast, the second practice involves an expatriate mothers' community created through participation in linked blogs, which is reinforced by communication on a range of other social media platforms. Where the Facebook groups are closed, semiprivate spaces with gatekeepers, these expat networks are open and public, and actively seek new interactions through linking strategies and reciprocity. Where the Facebook groups are grounded in a specific locality, the blogging networks are rootless and mobile, which creates a supportive community that expat mothers can take with them as they move across the world. As an Australian mother in China notes, "You'll be amazed at how comforting it is to know online, nothing has changed" (Webb).

These two relational systems are not mutually exclusive: a mother may be a member of both a closed Facebook group for mothers of the same migrant background, as well as a member of an expatriate mother blogging community. Nevertheless, they are working on contrasting logics: rootedness after rupture versus continuous connectivity and mobility; privacy and boundaries versus links and public space; and national, ethnic, or linguistic identity bonds versus expatriate identities. The discussion below illustrates some of the similarities and differences in these distinct approaches.

Mothering in the Diaspora: Facebook Groups

Local mothers' Facebook groups based on common ethnic, national, or linguistic ties are a growing phenomenon. In Sydney, Australia, for example, a 2016 search revealed nearly eighty such groups, covering over thirty nationalities, ethnicities, and linguistic groups, with over fifteen thousand members between them. Some groups had over one thousand members, some as few as two, with the average membership around two hundred. About half were Sydney-wide (e.g., South African Mums in Sydney), and half focused on smaller, local areas (e.g., South African Mums in the Hills District). These figures are no doubt an underestimation, as searching Facebook groups is difficult because of the wide variety of languages used in the group names and multiple terms used for "mother" in all languages; the number of geographical areas within Sydney and lack of consistency in naming practices around them; the limitations of the Facebook search facility as well as the privacy settings of groups which hinder verification; and, finally, the limitations implied by focusing exclusively on Facebook groups when Facebook is not uniformly popular in all migrant populations. Although still dominated by the English language, groups increasingly use their home language in the group title or group description, such as "Polskie Mamy w Sydney"[1] and אמא-פורג - תוהמא תוקוניתל סבידני.[2] Similar groups can be found in many cities worldwide, and it is clear that many migrant mothers choose to join online groups where they will be in contact with other mothers from the same ethnic, national, or linguistic background.

In an online survey I conducted in 2015 of 246 mothers of young children living in countries not of their birth or upbringing, the most common reason given for joining this kind of group was predominantly a desire to "connect with people like me."[3] "Like me" meant people who shared an identity (as mothers, fellow nationals, or mothers of colour), a situation (as people living away from family or living "here"), a common language, common values or sense of humour, or a shared cultural background or "frame of reference." This desire to connect is partly a rational "information foraging" strategy (Pirolli); people "like them" have access to the specific information they need to adapt to their new situation, namely information about local services and activities. As one British mother in the United Arab Emirates writes, "It's a relief to have someone to ask questions to when you are clueless and friendless in a strange country."

It is also a social strategy: a desire for reciprocal interaction with people likely to understand the challenges that they face and, therefore, provide emotional support through ongoing social relations. Respondents expressed a strong desire to use the online groups to form offline friendships too, and it was sometimes a source of disappointment if that did not happen. One British mother in Australia writes, "I plan on meeting up with them and being able to create a new version of the 'village'," while a Danish mother in the United States reflects, "I wish it had helped me more socially."

This combination of access to practical information, online emotional support, and offline friendships is critical to a reduced sense of isolation, the key outcome reported by the mothers. One British mother in Bulgaria writes:

> It has saved my sanity. It has given me and my children a social life, access to support and information. It has given me a space to feel validated and understood / accepted especially in countries where my cultural parenting choices are considered unusual or irresponsible. It has exposed me to a wide range of attitudes and approaches and helped me to feel more confident as a mother. It has

given us things to do on days that were strange and empty in a new country.

Mothers in these closed Facebook groups create bonds and roots in their new environment as they seek information and friendship in newly established networks, which mitigates the upheavals caused by migration and new motherhood.

Linked Blogs and Beyond: #myexpatfamily

The second practice shares some characteristics with the Facebook groups but is much more open. One example is #myexpatfamily, a monthly "linky" coordinated by a British mother living in the Seychelles (Howell). Each month, "Seychelles Mama" invites bloggers to post a link to one of their own posts in a group post. Contributors are encouraged to read and comment on each other's posts, which links this blogging community in a series of conversations. Blogging's role in creating online communities has been contested but is increasingly accepted (Blanchard; Webb and Lee). In the analysis of three monthly #myexpatfamily linky posts, containing eighty-one posts by forty-four bloggers[4] and a total of 1,427 comments, I encountered clear examples of tools and themes linking the bloggers together in a supportive community of peers.

Self-identification as an "expat" implies a connection with a collective migrant identity linked implicitly or explicitly with notions of whiteness, mobility, and privilege, and it may override, or work in tandem with, individual national identities (Fechter and Walsh 1200). Participants in the #myexpatfamily linky originate mostly from the UK (57 percent), the U.S. (23 percent) and Australia (9 percent); the rest come from mainland European countries (13 percent), the Philippines (2 percent), and Canada (2 percent). The bloggers' current countries of residence are more varied, but the most common locations are also the UK (16 percent), France (13.6 percent), the U.S. (11 percent), the United Arab Emirates (9 percent), Australia (7 percent), and European countries other than France and the UK (18 percent). Half of the bloggers reference their motherhood or family in their blog's name, such as "Mum Turned Mom," "Expatrimummy," and "Tiny Expats." Almost without exception, the blog's introduction focuses on the writer's family, migration story, and identity as a mother away from home. Some of the blogs have commercial elements and operate as a showcase for the skills of women working as freelance writers, or for the sale of products, such as books developed from the blogs.

The blogs reveal concerns about social isolation, displacement from home and support networks, as well as dealing with unfamiliar systems and cultural differences. The strategies for interaction employed through the blogs and their linked presences on other social media platforms exemplify Etienne Pelaprat and Barry Brown's concept of "reciprocity" as the basis for social relations online. The reciprocal interactions create social relations, which draw the mothers into relationships with one another to counteract their social isolation. The interactions also create opportunities for recognition that provide emotional resources (and reassurances) for navigating their path through unfamiliar territory.

The isolation expressed by these bloggers is a result of both physical and psychological distance. They describe feeling physically distant from their family and friendship networks, and also from the place that they call home. They indicate a sense of psychological estrangement from their family and friends, who are not "expats," as well as from their nonexpat local networks. One blogger describes the experience of settling in a new place with no local connections as "floating all alone in space" (Gustafson). There is a sense that their experience is distinctive—one that only other expat mothers could understand. The majority of the bloggers in this sample are stay-at-home mothers, or they are self-employed, or they balance caring responsibilities with freelance or casual work. The lack of opportunity to form networks through work colleagues, unlike their male partners, adds to their isolation. There are numerous references to "typical expat experiences" and a sense of relief in finding a network of people who understand. One strategy employed by these mothers, who describe feeling isolated both in their new environment and from their old one, is to create a community of mothers online who "get it"—a group who can provide reciprocal recognition through online interaction.

Almost all the blogs invite readers to connect with them on

other social media platforms, most often Twitter, followed by Instagram, Facebook, and Pinterest. These connections facilitate participation in collaborative social media activities beyond the blog linkies, such as the following: #myexpatfamily twitter chats (facilitated conversations at a specified time); a #myexpatfamily Instagram rotation curation account (where different expats run the account each week, posting pictures from their expat life); and a collaborative #myexpatfamily Pinterest board. By participating in these group activities across different platforms, the expat mothers are creating and expressing their identities as expat mothers within an open community of expat mothers; they are creating cross-platform opportunities for reciprocal interaction and recognition, and weaving webs of support, or what Barbara Ley has termed a "transmediated storytelling and support culture tapestry" (Ley 36).

Reciprocal actions online are important "as a powerful way of publically acknowledging others—recognition through reciprocation" (Pelaprat and Brown). The expat mother bloggers engage in multiple forms of these reciprocal actions, including "tagging," commenting, and retweeting links to blog posts. In one example, a blogger writes a post on the idea of "home" and tags other bloggers in the post to suggest that they write a post on the same topic. This creates a trail of thematically linked posts across blogs and encourages the "tagged" people to comment on the original post, thereby creating new opportunities for interaction.

The comment function displays the affective side of community building through interaction. Many of the bloggers assiduously reply to every comment left on their posts to create reciprocal exchanges. Commenters empathize, share their own experiences, offer suggestions, and show their appreciation for the photos, humour, information or openness displayed in a given post: "A lovely post! I completely agree that you only really form the attachment to home when you leave it. Best of luck for the move to south africa, and I hope it becomes your Home soon enough. #myexpatfamily" (Mommy on My Mind). The mothers in exchanges such as these echo Lori Lopez's finding that in blog comments "women are validating each other, displaying active listening and defining their own community" (742). The comments are also a space where further reciprocity is fostered: commenters link to or reference their own blogs or projects and invite people to get involved, cite a blog post as inspiration for their next post, or request permission to reproduce the post on their own site.

One of the core topics addressed by the expat mothers' blogs is the experience of navigating unfamiliar systems and cultural differences. Many of the bloggers reflect on the differences between "home" and "here" in such areas as food, education, childrearing, pregnancy and birth experiences, and housing. In contrast to the closed Facebook groups outlined above, where migrant mothers are primarily looking for local knowledge from other mothers to help them navigate unfamiliar systems, here the participants are looking for recognition, for validation that finding one's way in unfamiliar territory or managing conflicting mothering practices can be hard as well as potentially invigorating. They find this recognition primarily through the comments left by other expat mothers. Those comments may be a simple "how interesting" or "I so hear you," which extends recognition, sympathy or empathy. The bloggers may use the comment space to share a joke with one another about the (over)importance of a cup of tea in "British culture," or to share their own experiences or offer advice: "It's blogs like yours (and posts like this) that have shown me that I'm not going crazy, I'm not doing anything wrong, I'm just slowly adjusting to this new life I chose!" (Winter).

CONCLUSION

The closed Facebook groups and open blog networks have much in common with each other: they are communities of mothers, created by mothers, in the context of migration. They provide evidence of migrant mothers' resilience and resourcefulness in building the social capital that they need to survive and flourish in their new environment. Although the groups and blog networks may be examples of mothers' "community-building in the classic oral tradition, harkening to a time when women shared stories between each other instead of relying on institutions or male experts" (Lopez 743), it is also important to situate them in contemporary internet behaviours of information foraging and the quest for social relations through reciprocal interaction.

The blogs and Facebook groups highlight migrant mothers' daily concerns, habits, and reflections, and invite reciprocal interaction from other mothers. By posting on topics of common interest, they create opportunities for conversation, reassurance, and emotional support; each post is the first move "in a series of turn-taking exchanges that form social bonds of diverse kinds" (Pelaprat and Brown). In this way, migrant mothers become visible within a community, share experiences, and have their experiences and contemplations reflected back with empathy. In co-creating these online communities, mothers become a valuable resource for one another in the context of migration.

The public nature of the expatriate mothers' blogging community provides an opportunity to create their own narrative about their experiences, thereby forming an alternative discourse to those found elsewhere, both those characterised by Fechter as contributing to "the discursive vilification of colonial and contemporary expatriate wives" as idle, hedonistic and socially and racially divisive (Fechter 1294), as well as the more generic controlling discourses of motherhood (Douglas and Michaels). In the privacy of the closed groups, mothers emphasize information, advice, and friendship.

The blogging networks fit well with the concept of "connected migrants" (Diminescu, "The Connected Migrant"). These migrant mothers create online support networks, which become part of their "culture of bonds" that they can take with them as they move about the world. By contrast, migrant mothers use closed groups to put down new roots in a new locality and thereby demonstrate the limitations of the bonds that they bring with them and the importance of online connections in local as well as global contexts. The co-existence of these two social media practices among migrant mothers highlights the impact of rupture as well as the importance of connectivity to personal and collective migrant mothers' identities.

NOTES

[1]Polish mothers in Sydney.

[2]Mother and baby group in Sydney.
[3]The mothers were living across twenty-eight different countries, with the largest numbers in Australia and the UK.
[4]I excluded five posts by bloggers who were not mothers or who provided insufficient contextual information for analysis.

WORKS CITED

Arnold, Lorin Basden. "10 Years Out: Presence and Absence in a Long-Term Online Mothers' Community." *Motherhood Online*, edited by M. Moravec, Cambridge Scholars Publishing, 2011, pp. 73-96.

Barclay, Lesley, and Diane Kent. "Recent Immigration and the Misery of Motherhood: A Discussion of Pertinent Issues." *Midwifery*, vol. 14, no. 1, 1998, pp. 4-9.

Bartholomew, Mitchell K., et al. "New Parents' Facebook Use at the Transition to Parenthood." *Family Relations*, vol. 61, no. 3, 2012, pp. 455-469.

Benza, Sandra, and Pranee Liamputtong. "Pregnancy, Childbirth and Motherhood: A Meta-Synthesis of the Lived Experiences of Immigrant Women." *Midwifery*, vol. 30, no. 6, 2014, pp. 575-84.

Bernal, Victoria. *Nation as Network: Diaspora, Cyberspace, and Citizenship*. The University of Chicago Press, 2014.

Blanchard, Anita. "Blogs as Virtual Communities: Identifying a Sense of Community in the Julie/Julia Project." *University of Minnesota Libraries*, Regents of the University of Minnesota, 2004, conservancy.umn.edu/bitstream/handle/11299/172837/Blanchard_Blogs%20as%20Virtual%20Communities.pdf?sequence=1&isAllowed=y. Accessed 25 Aug. 2016.

Borda, Jennifer, L. "Blurred Boundaries in the Mommy Blogosphere." *The Motherhood Business: Consumption, Communication, and Privilege*, edited by Charlotte Kroløkke, University of Alabama Press, 2015, pp. 121-50.

Brinkerhoff, Jennifer M. *Digital Diasporas: Identity and Transnational Engagement*. Cambridge University Press, 2009.

DeSouza, Ruth. *New Spaces and Possibilities: The Adjustment to Parenthood for New Migrant Mothers*: Families Commission, 2006.

DeSouza, Ruth. "Transforming Possibilities of Care: Goan Migrant Motherhood in New Zealand.: *Contemporary Nurse: A Journal for the Australian Nursing Profession,* vol. 20, no. 1, 2005, pp. 87-101.

Diminescu, Dana. "The Connected Migrant: An Epistemological Manifesto." *Social Science Information,* vol. 47, no. 4, 2008, 565-579.

Diminescu, Dana. "Introduction: Digital Methods for the Exploration, Analysis and Mapping of E-Diasporas." *Social Science Information,* vol. 51, no. 4, 2012, pp. 451-458.

Douglas, Susan J, and Meredith W Michaels. *The Mommy Myth: The Idealization of Motherhood and How It Has Undermined All Women.* Free Press, 2004.

Drentea, Patricia, and Jennifer L. Moren-Cross. "Social Capital and Social Support on the Web: The Case of an Internet Mother Site." *Sociology of Health & Illness,* vol. 27, no. 7, 2005, pp. 920-943.

Dunham, Philip J., et al. "Computer-Mediated Social Support: Single Young Mothers as a Model System." *American Journal of Community Psychology,* vol. 26, no. 2, 1998, pp. 281-306.

Fechter, Anne-Meike. "Gender, Empire, Global Capitalism: Colonial and Corporate Expatriate Wives." *Journal of Ethnic and Migration Studies,* vol. 36, no. 8, 2010, pp. 1279-1297.

Fechter, Anne-Meike, and Katie Walsh. "Examining 'Expatriate' Continuities: Postcolonial Approaches to Mobile Professionals." *Journal of Ethnic and Migration Studies,* vol. 36, no. 8, 2010, 1197-210.

Friedman, May, and Shana L. Calixte, editors. *Mothering and Blogging: The Radical Act of the Mommyblog.* Demeter Press, 2009.

Gibson, Lorna, and Vicki L. Hanson. "Digital Motherhood." *Chi '13 Proceedings of the SIGCHIConference on Human Factors in Computing Systems.* New York: Association for Computing Machinery, 2013, pp. 313-322.

Greschke, Heike Mónika. "Make Yourself at Home in www.cibervalle.com – Meanings of Proximity & Togetherness in the Era of 'Broadband Society.'" *Migration, Diaspora, and Information Technology in Global Societies,*edited by Leopoldina Fortunati et al., Routledge, 2012, pp. 124-138.

Gustafson, Erin. "Size Matters." *Oregon Girl Around the World,* 2015, oregongirlaroundtheworld.com/2015/03/11/size-matters/. Accessed 25 Aug. 2016.

Hoang, H. T. et al. "Having a Baby in the New Land: A Qualitative Exploration of the Experiences of Asian Migrants in Rural Tasmania, Australia." *Rural & Remote Health*, vol. 9, no. 1, 2009, pp. 1084-1084.

Howell, Chantelle. "My Expat Family Linky." *Seychelles Mama,* 2016, www.seychellesmama.com. Accessed 25 Aug. 2016.

Jensen, Tracey. "Mumsnetiquette: Online Affect within Parenting Culture." *Privilege, Agency and Affect*, edited by Claire Maxwell and Peter Aggleton, Palgrave Macmillan, 2013, pp. 127-45.

Kim, Jinyoung, et al. *Korean Mothers' Kakaostory Use and Its Relationship to Psychological Well-Being. First Monday,* First Monday, 2015, firstmonday.org/ojs/index.php/fm/article/view/5576/4379. Accessed 25 Aug. 2016.

Ley, Barbara L. "Beyond Discussion Forums: The Transmediated Support Culture of an Online Pregnancy and Mothering Group." *Motherhood Online,* edited by M. Moravec, Cambridge Scholars Publishing, 2011, pp. 23-44.

Lopez, Lori Kido. "The Radical Act of 'Mommy Blogging': Redefining Motherhood through the Blogosphere." *New Media & Society*, vol. 11, no. 5, 2009, pp. 729-747.

Madge, Clare, and Henrietta O'Connor. "Parenting Gone Wired: Empowerment of New Mothers on the Internet?" *Social & Cultural Geography*, vol. 7, no. 2, 2006, pp. 199-220.

Madianou, Mirca. "Migration and the Accentuated Ambivalence of Motherhood: The Role of Icts in Filipino Transnational Families." *Global Networks*, vol. 12, no. 3, 2012, 277-295.

Manohar, Namita N. and Erika Busse-Cárdenas. "Valuing 'Good' Motherhood in Migration: The Experiences of Indian Professional Wives in America and Peruvian Working-Class Wives Left Behind in Peru." *Journal of the Motherhood Initiative for Research and Community Involvement*, vol. 2, no. 2, 2011, pp. 175-95.

Moravec, M, editor. *Motherhood Online.* Cambridge Scholars Publisher, 2011.

O' Reilly, Andrea. "Outlaw(Ing) Motherhood: A Theory and Politic of Maternal Empowerment for the Twenty-First Century."

Hecate, vol. 36, no. 1-2, 2010, pp. 17-29.

Mummy on My Mind (user name). Comment on "A Bittersweet Homecoming," *Expat Partner Survival*, WordPress, 11 Jun 2015, 9:51 a.m., expatpartnersurvival.com/2015/06/11/a-bittersweet-homecoming/. Accessed 29 Aug. 2016

Pelaprat, Etienne, & Barry Brown. "Reciprocity: Understanding online social relations." *First Monday* [Online], vol. 17, no. 10, 2012. Accessed. 16 Nov. 2015

Pirolli, P. *Information Foraging Theory:Adaptive Interaction with Information*. Oxford University Press, 2007.

Rogan, F., et al. "'Becoming a Mother'—Developing a New Theory of Early Motherhood." *Journal of Advanced Nursing*, vol. 25, no. 5, 1997, pp. 877-885.

Ryan, L., et al. "'The Distance between Us': A Comparative Examination of the Technical, Spatial and Temporal Dimensions of the Transnational Social Relationships of Highly Skilled Migrants." *Global Networks*, vol. 15, no. 2, 2015, vol. 198-216. Print

Su, Chang, and Michaela Hynie. "Effects of Life Stress, Social Support, and Cultural Norms on Parenting Styles among Mainland Chinese, European Canadian, and Chinese Canadian Immigrant Mothers." *Journal of Cross-Cultural Psychology*, vol. 42, no. 6, 2011, pp. 944-962.

Wang, Gan. "'Net-Moms'—a New Place and a New Identity: Parenting Discussion Forums on the Internet in China." *Provincial China*, vol. 8, no. 1, 2003, pp. 78-88.

Ward, Catherine. "Migrant Mothers and the Role of Social Support When Child Rearing." *Contemporary Nurse*, vol. 16, no. 1-2, 2004, pp. 74-85.

Webb, Lynne M, and Brittney S Lee. "Mommy Blogs: The Centrality of Community in the Performance of Online Maternity." *Motherhood Online*, edited by M. Moravec, Cambridge Scholar Publishing, 2011, pp. 244-257.

Webb, Nicole. Comment on "A Bittersweet Homecoming," *Expat Partner Survival*, WordPress, 15 July 2015, 12:56 p.m., expatpartnersurvival.com/2015/06/11/a-bittersweet-homecoming/. Accessed 25 Aug. 2016.

Webb, Nicole. "Week One: Living in China." *Mint Mocha Musings*, 2014, mintmochamusings.com/living-in-china/. Accessed

18 Feb. 2016.

Winter, Anne. Comment on "Nobody Told Me Culture Shock Could Be So Debilitating," *Expat Life (with a Double Buggy)*, 7 Jul. 2015, 9:10 p.m. lifewithadoublebuggy.blogspot.com. au/2015/07/nobody-told-me-culture-shock-could-be.html. Accessed 29 Aug. 2016.

6.
Mothers of Honor

Intentional Creation of Pregnancy, Birth, and Postpartum Support

TARA STAMM, CASEY YU, AND STEPHANIE KENNEDY

A LTHOUGH IT IS COMMON for women to prepare for their transition to marriage with the support of a maid of honor, preparation for the transition to motherhood rarely has such an intentionally created support system. However, a woman's experiences during pregnancy, birth, and the postpartum period also require practical and emotional support, especially for those who experience traumatic births. Coining the term "mothers of honor" to describe the women who voluntarily assist mothers with the specific challenges of traumatic births, this chapter is a co-constructed autobiography exploring the importance of the mothering support given to three women after traumatic, emergent Caesarean deliveries, and how that support has been paid forward through the use of social media. Although the current chapter focuses on emergent, Caesarean deliveries, the content presented and the mothers of honor construct are also relevant to women who experience traumatic births more broadly, including births that deviate from the intended birth plan, involve prolonged labour or adverse intervention effects, or have poor outcomes for either mother or child. We present a review of relevant literature and conduct a critical analysis of how each author accessed her mother(s) of honor and later served in this capacity for others. Future research directions are also suggested.

RATES OF CAESAREAN DELIVERY IN THE U.S. AND CANADA

The Caesarean delivery rate in the United States has increased more than sevenfold in the past five decades—from just 4.5 percent in 1965 to over 30 percent in 2014 (Stadtlander 71; Taffel et al. 955). In Canada, rates have similarly risen from 18.7 percent in 1997 to 27.5 percent in 2014 (Canadian Institute for Health Information). Although Caesarean delivery is recommended for some high-risk pregnancies (e.g., maternal medical conditions, fetal positioning, and multiple fetuses), the World Health Organization suggests that Caesarean section rates in excess of 10 percent are not associated with reduced maternal or newborn mortality at the population level (1). Therefore, the dramatic increase in the prevalence of Caesarean delivery cannot be explicitly associated with medical need. Rather, it is likely associated with a constellation of individual and structural factors, ranging from the adverse effects of common labour interventions (e.g., slowing of labour in the wake of an epidural) and patient preference to efficiency demands placed on medical providers by reimbursement schedules and doctors' desire for greater work-life balance (Goer et al. 26). Currently, more than 60 percent of first-time Caesareans are unplanned, and women most often identify their medical provider as the primary decision maker (Declercq et al. 23).

THE RELATIONSHIP BETWEEN CAESAREAN DELIVERY AND NEGATIVE OUTCOMES

Complicated birth experiences, including emergent Caesarean deliveries, have been linked to a range of physical and mental health issues, feelings of isolation, and mother-child bonding challenges (Goer et al. 26; Lowe 135; Moehler et al. 273). Maternal morbidity and mortality rates are elevated; women who deliver by Caesarean are more likely to suffer an amniotic fluid embolism, a uterine rupture, an emergent hysterectomy, and a range of adverse surgical effects (Caughey et al. 179). These unintended physical consequences may affect subsequent pregnancies and limit future birthing options (Stadtlander 71). Furthermore, the Caesarean birth process typically limits or even eliminates immediate skin-to-skin contact between mother and baby in the operating room, and may prolong separation while a mother is sedated or otherwise recovering (Magee et al. 690). The U.S. Department of Health and

Human Services reports an inverse relationship between breast-feeding and Caesarean sections, as the physical recovery process may delay or complicate the initiation of successful breastfeeding (1). Thus, Caesarean delivery may negatively affect attachment or breastfeeding in the postpartum period (Prior et al. 1115; Shealy et al. 4).

Emergent Caesarean births are also associated with increased incidence and prevalence of post-traumatic stress (Garthus-Niegel et al. 7; Olde et al. 7). A variety of predisposing factors have been identified (e.g., pre-existing mental health issues and the level of support received), that intersect with the experience of birth and availability of postpartum support. However, support is typically measured solely in terms of the intimate partner relationship. Although the correlation between delivery method and postpartum depression (PPD) (Carter et al. 328) is less clear, Houston et al. have found that levels of PPD were highest for those who delivered via Caesarean after expressing a strong desire for a vaginal birth (229.e4). Houston et al. have hypothesized that women who place emotional value on vaginal delivery and undergo an emergent Caesarean are at increased risk for postpartum emotional and mental health challenges (229.e4).

SOCIAL MEDIA AS SOCIAL SUPPORT

Several authors have examined women's thoughts, feelings, and perceived partner support after a Caesarean delivery (e.g., Beck 306; Elmir et al. 2145; Lemola et al. 200); however, less is known about how support is accessed through online social networks, especially within online communities for mothers. The impact of this type of support on health and wellness is important to understand, as social media groups can be used as a postpartum intervention (McDaniel et al. 1509). Authors conducting systematic reviews of peer-based Internet support groups suggest marginal positive effects on coping, connectedness, and general mental health (Gabbert et al. 1675; Niela-Vilan 1534). The authors note that the most pronounced effects are in homogenous groups of parents with sick or disabled children. We have found no examinations of the effects of this type of social media intervention for women who experienced an emergent Caesarean or any other type of traumatic birth.

The social and emotional benefits of social media or Internet-based support groups for women who have experienced a traumatic or surgical birth are also largely unexplored. The post-traumatic-growth construct suggests that most people who experience trauma are resilient—in that they will make meaning from traumatic events—and the process of recovery will alter their sense of self and interpersonal relationships in a positive way (Tedeschi et al 5). Ervin Staub and Johanna Vollhardt suggest that a key facet of the post-traumatic-growth construct is offering assistance to others in the aftermath of trauma (270). Dubbed "altruism born of suffering," this phenomenon explains how some people transform their personal suffering into a vehicle to help others. Although empirical evidence is limited, those who engage in this type of altruism appear to have greater psychological recovery (272). Evaluations of this construct, however, have been limited to experiences of family violence, crime, or natural disaster, and how survivors help others in their community. Whether and how altruism born of suffering occurs in the context of social media is currently unexamined. We argue that women who undergo a traumatic birth, however that is defined, also engage in altruism born of suffering and that these activities, which promote growth and resilience, are facilitated by the use of social media communication.

Trigger Warning

This chapter presents emotionally charged autobiographical narratives that describe three women's reactions to a traumatic, emergent Caesarean birth experience. Infant loss is also discussed. These narratives may elicit a strong emotional reaction from readers. A resource guide for accessing support is included at the end of the chapter.

CASE VIGNETTES

The current study used co-constructed autobiography to examine this issue (Taylor et al. 1). This method allowed us to apply a critical lens to our own and one another's personal experiences, while situating those experiences within a broader cultural narrative.

Autobiography and co-constructed narrative were appropriate methods for this study as little is known about whether and how women access social media support in the wake of an emergent Caesarean delivery, and the intensity of emotion implicit in each autobiography leant itself to therapeutic co-construction of the larger narrative (Ellis et al. 1). We explored the "mothers of honor" construct through the lens of three unique but interrelated birthing experiences. We defined "mothers of honor" as the confluence of two relationships. In the first relationship, we received support from mothers who also experienced an emergent Caesarean. In the second, we served in this role, via social media, for other mothers in the wake of their emergent Caesarean. Each author independently wrote about accessing support via social media before and after an emergent Caesarean delivery and how that support was given to other mothers who endured similar hardships. Then, each narrative was discussed among the group, which allowed for the intersection of inquiry and emotion to guide case refinement. Each narrative focuses on a slightly different aspect of online social support and reflects individual perspectives on the meaning of the term "mothers of honor."

TARA

During my birth class, we played a card game. The cards were labelled with possible decision points (i.e., interventions) during labour. I had no idea a labouring woman would be asked to make so many choices. The goal of the game was to identify those things that I was not willing to compromise and to select three or four interventions that I felt would not diminish my birth experience. During this exercise, I ranked "relationship support" fairly low, as I thought that I would rather birth alone than endure an episiotomy. I hardly paid attention to discussions of Caesarean birth. I thought my knowledge, prestige, financial resources, and overall excellent health would enable me to avoid most medical interventions—especially a scalpel.

By thirty-five weeks, however, I had gained almost one hundred pounds. My blood pressure was registering high, and I had protein in my urine, which is an early indicator of kidney failure. The midwife assured my husband and me that this was no big deal and that I should go to the hospital to have a doctor check my blood pressure just to be safe. Blissfully unaware of our circumstances, we left the jets on the hot tub running, headed to the neonatal ward, and innocently told the nurses that we needed to complete our pre-labour paperwork, and I said, "Oh! And my doctor asked that my blood pressure be checked again." After the nurses checked and rechecked my blood pressure, my obstetrician came into the room still wearing her surgical scrubs. She told us that I would need to stay at the hospital until the baby came. Confused, my husband asked, "What's the big deal? Don't people walk around with high blood pressure all the time?" The doctor looked my husband directly in the eyes and said, "Sir, your wife is very, very ill and she could die. She will remain in the hospital until she gives birth." Stunned, we asked for a few minutes of privacy. We cried. We cried about the loss of the birth we wanted, we cried because we had not finished decorating the nursery, we cried that we would be separated for much of the few weeks we had left together as a family of two. We cried because we were scared.

My husband stayed with me in the hospital that first night. In the middle of the night, I woke him up and said, "Please call them. Call everyone. Tell them we need help." The next day, he called in every resource, favour, and friend to begin scheduling any and all assistance that we might need. All the mothers, mothers-in-law, and stepmothers were to come after the birth. I had manicures, pedicures, waxes, facials, and haircuts in my hospital bed. I taught and attended classes via Skype during working hours. Even my dog came for a few hours, which to my obstetrician's delight, provided the lowest blood pressure readings in any twenty-four hour period.

I continued to gain around six pounds per day. On-call doctors put heavy pressure on us to immediately elect a Caesarean, as I was putting my life in danger by waiting. However, we chose to wait, as we preferred to be in the hospital with the baby inside over delivering a baby directly into the NICU. After three weeks of hospital bedrest, the fetal development specialist gave the thumbs up and said the baby's lungs were fully developed. The acupuncturist came and induced labour with tiny needles that put downward pressure on my abdomen. Along with our doula, we still had a glimmer of hope for a vaginal, unmedicated birth.

Our baby was delivered two days later by abdominal incision. I was defeated—physically, emotionally, mentally, psychologically. All reserves were depleted. My body was devastated, and the tears began. As I shuffled around my house unable to stand, sit, or hold my baby without immense pain, I cried. I did not stop crying for another ten months. This was not my birth; this was not my baby; this was not my body.

Day and night, I texted my mother of honor who was two years out from her own unwanted Caesarean delivery. She taught my husband to use the sheets from the bed to pull me gently to a sitting position, so I could feed the baby. She demonstrated how to bounce a fussy infant without shooting pain through my abdomen. She assured me that I would one day be mostly pain free and would no longer need to sleep in a recliner. She agreed that it is indeed awful how all underwear fit perfectly to aggravate the scar. She did all of this in the deepest, darkest hours of the night when the pain and emotions were most overwhelming.

I helped her once, too, before we became mothers. I held her wedding gown off the bathroom floor and handed her a powder compact before taking her photograph. In comparison, my contribution seems insignificant. Cultural norms dictate a personal assistant for a woman getting married, yet new parents are supposed to fend for themselves when bringing a new baby home from the hospital—even when one of those parents is recovering from abdominal surgery.

Five weeks after my baby was delivered, I found the International Caesarean Awareness Network (ICAN) group on Facebook. I went to a local meeting, where I sat in a stuffy room with fifteen other women and blurted the unsayable: my birth was the worst thing that had ever happened to me. No one shifted; no one looked away; no one tried to talk me off the ledge. They nodded—empathy and agreement in their eyes. They said the following: "what happened to you was awful"; "you can mourn your birth"; "we've been there"; "we too hurt for you." And that's how my Caesarean birth recovery began.

In those first few months postpartum, I only got out of bed for necessary engagements. My husband arranged for my therapist to see me at home. I hated going to breastfeeding support where the other mothers were able to walk into a room upright carrying their own babies. For me, a walk to the mailbox was a victory. But the women in the ICAN Facebook group were always there—sharing, vulnerable, trying. My mother of honor certainly guided me in those first few weeks, but four years and a cross-country move later, I depend on the women online for daily encouragement and support. I check in on them daily and offer thoughts or advice where I think I can be of assistance. I stay engaged with the online group because I want the new mothers, those who are freshly experiencing trauma, to know that the community is deep and reaches out to them long after the physical scars heal.

CASEY

William was my third ride at the motherhood rodeo. My first two children were born without much fanfare—hospital births with my loved ones holding my legs as I pushed until they emerged, crying at their disruption. I expected the same with William, but early on we discovered that William was growing too slowly. At twenty weeks, my blood pressure skyrocketed. At twenty-four weeks, I was placed on bedrest with severe superimposed preeclampsia. I lay on my side for eight weeks until my body could take no more. He was delivered via Caesarean at thirty-two weeks and weighed only three pounds, two ounces. William spent eight weeks in the NICU while I visited him daily, pumped milk around the clock, and sought out my mothers of honor for support.

The Ranch developed as an offshoot of a parenting playgroup on Facebook. In the Ranch, mothers explore the rawer and uncomfortable aspects of parenting: why was breastfeeding so emotionally draining? What if our children hated us? How do you negotiate love, sex, and intimacy in a range of relationships? Over time, these discussions built a community of moms who mothered one another—in the way we wanted and needed to be cared for. Halfway through my pregnancy, I sat in my cubicle at school and cried while messaging Melissa that I could not feel William move. She showed up with a handheld Doppler, and held my hand and cried with me when she found William's heartbeat pounding fast and strong. On bedrest, one of my mothers of honor would pick me up every week and come with me to the doctor, where William's size and growth were monitored. This happened every week for eight weeks without fail. They organized a "bedrest baby shower," with gift cards to local restaurants, toys for my older kids to play with, and yarn for my knitting. The day I was admitted to the hospital for William's birth, the messages that I received were heartwarming and enveloping, and wrapped me in love and comfort.

After William's birth, I saw him momentarily before he was whisked away to the NICU. I sat alone in my room and listened to newborns crying down the hall. Leslee, whose daughter was born four years earlier via Caesarean, came to visit me. Choking my back tears, I said, "I still feel pregnant. It's like my body didn't realize I had a baby. I never pushed. It still feels like he's inside me, Leslee." I cried and cried. "I know," she said, hugging and crying with me. "I know. And it's not fair. I'm so sorry," Leslee repeated. It was Mother's Day in 2013, and I was a new mother with no baby. Just a breastpump and tiny paper flowers Leslee's daughter made for me.

Once I left the hospital, my mothers of honor took turns bringing my husband and me food and cookies as we visited the NICU daily. Every Wednesday, moms got together for knit night, and not one soul batted an eye as I hooked myself up to a noisy breastpump in the coffee shop. I was determined to pump on schedule so that I could make the milk that would bring this child home into all of our arms. They began to chant a mantra with me—"Free Will"—and followed #freewill on Facebook. They changed their profile pictures to a pink shirt that had "Free Will" emblazoned on it. They cried with me in joy when on Independence Day 2013, he was finally released home to us. Will was free after spending fifty-six days in the NICU.

Will is two now, and my family has relocated to Dhaka, Bangladesh. I am 8,700 miles away from many of my mothers of honor, but I am incredibly fortunate to still have access to the Ranch via Facebook, and share our adventures in Bangladesh while staying connected to my support system back home. I knew that I needed to recreate this spirit of community here in Dhaka, which I have done with a group of expatriate mothers. Although we struggle like mothers all over the world, our challenges are now coloured much differently, as we parent internationally from the U.S., the UK, and Australia in Bangladesh.

I met Sonya a few months after my arrival in Dhaka. Originally from Texas, she had two girls and was pregnant with her third child, a boy. We eagerly awaited the birth of her third baby, Ian, and anticipated a truly joyous occasion. Sonya was scheduled to deliver Ian by Caesarean, and so we spent time talking about my Caesarean and what she should ask for—immediate skin-to-skin contact, a breastpump waiting in her room, and the chance to talk to her anesthesiologist about what medications were going into her IV drip. I was excited to take newborn photos and was glued to my phone waiting for Ian's arrival. But she called me the day after Ian was born. He was in trouble; his heart had a severe defect that the best hospitals in Bangladesh could not fix.

I packed my camera, got to the hospital, and sat with her because that's what my mothers of honor did for me. I sat with my friend. I held her hand and cried. I helped her assemble the breastpump. I researched med-evac helicopters and lamented the exorbitant costs. We stood outside the NICU window and watched Sonya put on sterile gear and softly rub her son's beautiful, beautiful scalp while he slept in the incubator. Instead of newborn photos of a baby at home, I took newborn photos of Sonya in a sterile gown, as she cradled Ian, sleeping in an isolette. They were finally able to secure admission from a hospital in Kuala Lumpur and transport him there for surgery. I hugged her fiercely before she left. Our Dhaka community waited for any photo, any sign of hope. We all loved Ian so much. We hoped against everything that he would make it and that the surgery would be successful and fix the holes in his heart. And when he died, a collective weight of grief fell on all of us. Now, we waited for them to come back to us for a traditional Muslim funeral and burial ceremony.

I shared this experience with the Ranch—all of my anger and frustration at a system unprepared to care for Ian and at the grave injustice of a life taken too young. My support system cried with me from afar and typed message after message of sadness and prayers. Even though they did not know Sonya, they mourned with her. They assured me that I was being a good friend in this time of indescribable grief, even though I felt as if I had done nothing or accomplished nothing. If I had not had my mothers of honor from the Ranch, I could not have done it at all. I learned to become a mother of honor by example—Melissa holding me while we listened for Will's heartbeat and Leslee hugging me tightly after my Caesarean with William. If I had not had that group of mothers, I would have stumbled, helpless and lost, using trial and error as my two leading guides. I was so lucky that in my time of need, my mothers of honor caught me, propped me up, and helped me gently fall as needed, cry as warranted, and love wholeheartedly, both when I had my Caesarean and when Sonya had hers.

STEPHANIE

I intended to give birth at home. I envisioned a warm birth tub and the support of a capable birth team. Unfortunately, my daughter was poorly positioned, and after many, many hours of labour at home, we transferred to the hospital for assistance. I laboured there for many more hours with limited progress. I accepted all the drugs. I negotiated a new plan with a doctor I had never met. And by breakfast the following morning, I was being wheeled into the OR.

The events of the OR move slowly in my mind: pushing and pulling sensations on my abdomen; heavy tools plunked unceremoniously on my chest behind the drape; the doctor's lilting Italian accent as he apologized for having perforated my bladder. But most vividly, I remember feeling the weight of my daughter on my chest, her still-sticky skin clinging to mine. I lay awake on that operating table for four hours; at first, I held my baby, then I watched her leave. I begged my husband to stay with me. We made up stories while we waited for the urologist to arrive to repair the damage. In my mind, birth smells like cauterized flesh.

I am told that I said goodbye to my husband at some point in that OR; that my friends anxiously drove past my house, wondering where we had gone; and that my doula never left my side. It's all sort of a blur to me, steeped in both gratitude and despair. People said a lot of things to me in those first few weeks, as I dragged a

Foley catheter around under a long dress. The words "death" and "die" came up often. Some thanked God, and others asked what I was thinking. "At least you have a healthy baby," they told me as I emptied the catheter bag into the toilet.

But my mother of honor whispered a different story. She told me that having a healthy baby is the most important outcome of birth but not the only important outcome. My story and my body also mattered; she allowed me to grieve the loss of the birth that I wanted while still being grateful for the care I received. She spoke of my experience only as a Caesarean birth or a Caesarean delivery. She made a face whenever someone said "C-section" or used the truly awful verb "sectioned." She confessed that after her own Caesarean, she struggled to think of herself as having given birth at all; that she still feels as though her babies were ripped from her abdomen.

She took me to an ICAN meeting a week or so postpartum. But my emotions were too raw, and I crumpled under the harsh fluorescent lights in the utilitarian conference room. I briefly contemplated becoming an admin of a homebirth Caesarean group on Facebook. I was six weeks postpartum—two weeks catheter-free—and felt my cheerful, pragmatic sensibility return. "I can do this," I mused to my baby as she nursed: "I can be of service to others." I was filled with a desperate urge to say all of the right things to these women, whom I knew were feeling guilty for not having a "natural" birth (whatever that means) and were likely being peppered with judgement and shame by their loved ones. But there were too many women hurting so badly, and I felt as if I were drowning. About the same time, an acquaintance emailed me out of the blue. She had just given birth to her second child and wanted to reach out in case I needed a place to vent or cry or question my choice to have a baby in the first place. Her births were straightforward, but she handled me kindly and expressed all the right outrage about my experience. I was so thankful to have this semi-stranger in my corner and even more thankful to not be sharing my experience in a group setting.

Over the next few months, many friends posted photos of their newborn babies on Facebook. I scoured the images for signs of complication. In addition to photos taken in the OR, I learned to detect other, more subtle tells: waiting days (or more) to post a photo; references to a long, hard labour or a last-minute change of plans; and streams of loved ones echoing that tired platitude—a healthy baby is all that matters. I reached out to these women one by one, some of whom I had not seen since we were little girls. Some were the partners of former students—women I have never met. I told them all what my mother of honor told me: a healthy baby matters, but they also matter. It is normal to feel sad and scared and happy and overwhelmed and angry and in love. It is completely normal to feel all of these things or none of these things.

Although I have received many thank-yous, periodically someone takes up the conversation in earnest. They tell stories of preeclampsia, induction, poorly placed epidurals, adverse reactions to Pitocin, and hemorrhage; stories about doctors who checked their watch and rubbed their eyes at 10:00 p.m., before suggesting a Caesarean for "failure to progress"; and stories of women denied skin-to-skin contact in the OR, who had their arms strapped down, and who were barely allowed to see their babies before they were whisked away for nonemergency tests. A woman whom I have never met told me that a nurse denied her request for a wheelchair two hours after surgery. Instead, the nurse suggested that she "get up out the bed" and walk to the NICU to hold her baby for the first time. A dear friend told me how she swelled so badly after surgery that she was unable to use her arms for days. She literally could not pick up her son from the bassinette, and she was worried that she would never fall in love with him because of how much pain she was in.

I cannot imagine telling these women that a healthy baby is all that matters, or labelling them as selfish or decadent for wanting more, wanting better. Yet each woman indicated that this sort of talk represented the bulk of the postpartum message: birth is hard and uncontrollable; birth plans are for spoiled first-world princesses; and mothering is about sacrifice. Even when the message came from their own mothers—many of whom also had Caesarean births—empathy was lacking. Care was only intentionally extended to the baby, and new mothers felt isolated and unhappy; they felt guilty for feeling so envious of the love being lavished on their sons and daughters.

I know that the specific events of my birth experience were, in some way, anomalous. And I am certainly grateful for the healthy baby girl I delivered. But in many ways, the love I feel as a mother grew in the context of other women, bolstered by their courage in the face of suffering. Although I cannot tell or read this story without tears, I tell it over and over again in the hope to validate some other woman's suffering. My mothers of honor extended care to me without hesitation and, together, we continue to create and recreate a counter-narrative for mothers in their time of greatest need.

DISCUSSION

The case vignettes detail the importance of the mothering support given to three women after traumatic, emergent Caesarean births, and how that support was paid forward in an intentional way via social media. Taken together, these vignettes provide support for the hypothesis that post-traumatic growth, resilience, and altruism are not uncommon responses to traumatic experiences. Furthermore, the deeper emotional undercurrents of our narratives suggest that the dynamic nature of adjustment in the wake of traumatic birth and highlight the interconnectedness of personal struggle with resilience. Although formal avenues of postpartum support are available in most communities (see Resources below), few face-to-face or online communities specifically address the unique needs of mothers in the wake of a traumatic birth experience. All three authors had some contact with ICAN; however, individual and group support was sought out via social media as a supplement or substitution for this formal contact. The diverse social media support networks created by each author are neither homogenous nor static, which underscores how Internet-based support can be tailored over time to meet specific needs as they arise.

Although we are years out from our birth experiences, writing and discussing these vignettes individually and as a group was extraordinarily difficult. We hesitated to write, to read and edit, to re-engage with those powerful feelings again. Furthermore, each of us had a role in the other birth experiences; we all three met at an ICAN meeting, and Tara served as Stephanie's mother of honor. Therefore, the editing process was also very emotional for us, as we reflected on the part that we had played in the events described. We wept for each other again and again. It was a challenge to step back into that space of fear and devastation while maintaining a focus on the strong communities we have helped to create. In the literature, suffering and resilience are often treated as discreet phenomena; however, our narratives suggest that post-traumatic stress and growth are intricately entwined, and often occur simultaneously. The "mothers of honor" construct also supports Staub and Vollhardt's notion of "altruism born of suffering." We sought to intercede in the lives of others to present an alternative narrative for those in need (270). The support we received and provided via social media was a powerful vehicle that helped us to move forward from our experiences of emergent Caesarean birth, both as individual women and as members of a broader community of mothers.

Several limitations of the current analysis warrant careful consideration. These three vignettes may not reflect general trends in women's access of support via social media in the wake of an emergent Caesarean birth, which is, of course, only one facet of the traumatic birth experience. Also, we share several characteristics that distinguish us in important ways from other women transitioning to motherhood. Although we were raised in different socioeconomic contexts, we self-identify as American, middle class, and heterosexual, and we each planned our pregnancies within the context of long-term married relationships. Furthermore, we were all pursuing doctoral-level education at the time of our emergent Caesarean and had partners who were deeply involved in the provision of emotional and instrumental support. These factors might have influenced our ability to seek out and engage social support via nontraditional Internet-based sources, as our collective privilege afforded us the time and the space to reflect on our birth experiences and explore our thoughts, feelings, and general mental health.

Despite these limitations, however, the current study highlights how three women accessed and engaged support through social media after an emergent Caesarean birth within online communities targeting the unique experiences and needs of mothers. As suggested in the literature review, little is known about this type of social support, including who is accessing it (and who is not), how online communities respond to new members, conflict, and change over time, and how this social support affects post-traumatic growth, maternal mental health, and the mother-baby bond. In general, more research is needed to explore the risks and benefits of engaging with other mothers in this manner—especially when communities are comprised of members who do not "know" each other nonvirtually. Accessing online support via social networks was clearly beneficial to the authors, and has potential for engaging mothers who live in remote locations or those who do not otherwise have access to a supportive social network in their lives. However, future research should seek out the counter-narrative and explore potential negative consequences of accessing this type of virtual support (e.g., conflicts with group members or negative emotional reactions). Exploring a diversity of voices and experiences will provide a more comprehensive understanding of the potential for social media support interventions in the wake of an emergent Caesarean delivery or other traumatic birth experiences.

RESOURCES

International Caesarean Awareness Network: www.ican-online. org/. ICAN's mission is to improve maternal-child health by preventing unnecessary Caesareans through education, providing support for Caesarean recovery, and promoting vaginal birth after Caesarean (VBAC). Local ICAN chapters and direct peer-to-peer support meetings can be accessed via Facebook.

Homebirth Caesarean: homebirth Caesarean.org/. Homebirth Caesarean provides support, resources, and awareness around planned out-of-hospital births that end in Caesareans. It serves mothers, birth professionals, and those interested in the conversation about empowered birth, and offers closed groups for both women who experience a Caesarean after planning a homebirth and for their partners are available via Facebook.

Postpartum Support International: www.postpartum.net. Postpartum Support International provides direct peer support to families, trains professionals, and provides a bridge to connect them. It offers local peer resources, "search and chat with an expert" functions, and online support groups for women, and includes a wealth of resources for understanding postpartum mental health issues and accessing supportive counselling. Resources for partners can be accessed at www.postpartum.net/family/tips-for-postpartum-dads-and-partners/.

Birthing from Within: www.birthingfromwithin.com/pages/birth-story-medicine. Birthing from Within supports women as they prepare for birth as a rite of passage. It also offers an online space called "Birth Story Medicine," which allows women to tell their stories in an effort to heal emotional birth trauma.

Solace for Mothers: www.solaceformothers.org/. Solace for Mothers supports for women who have experienced childbirth as traumatic, even if the birth experience is deemed "normal." Resources and online support groups are available.

Postpartum Progress: www.postpartumprogress.com/. Postpartum progress includes resources for women experiencing postpartum mood and anxiety disorders.

The Birth Trauma Association (UK): http://birthtraumaassociation. org.uk/. The Birth Trauma Association supports all women who have had a traumatic birth experience. It provides resources for obtaining emotional and physical postpartum support. A Facebook group is also available.

Share Pregnancy & Infant Loss Support: http://nationalshare. org/. Share Pregnancy & Infant Loss Support provides support and education for anyone who experiences the death of a baby. Open psychoeducational groups and closed groups for bereaved parents in English and Spanish can be accessed at http://nationalshare.org/fb-support-pages/.

WORKS CITED

Beck, Cheryl T. "A Metaethnography of Traumatic Childbirth

and its Aftermath: Amplifying Causal Looping." *Qualitative Health Research*, vol. 21, no. 3, 2011, pp. 301-311.

Carter, F.A., et al. "Caesarean Section and Postpartum Depression: A Review of the Evidence Examining the Link." *Psychosomatic Medicine*, vol. 68, no. 2, 2006, pp. 321-330.

Canadian Institute for Health Information (CIHI). *Health Indicators Interactive Tool*, CIHI, 2016, yourhealthsystem.cihi.ca/epub/search.jspa. Accessed 25 Aug. 2016.

Caughey, Aaron B, et al. "Safe Prevention of the Primary Caesarean Delivery." *American Journal of Obstetrics and Gynecology*, vol. 210, no. 3, 2014, pp. 179-193.

Declercq, Eugene R. et al. "Listening to Mothers III: Report of the Third National Survey of Women's Childbearing Experiences." *Childbirth Connection*, National Partnership for Women and Families 2013, www.childbirthconnection.org. Accessed 25 Aug. 2016.

Ellis, Carolyn, et al. "Autoethnography: An Overview." *Forum: Qualitative Social Research*, vol. 12, no. 1, 2011. *Research Gate*, doi: 10.1353/bio.0.0097.

Elmir, R., et al. "Women's Perceptions and Experiences of a Traumatic Birth: A Meta-Ethnography." *Journal of Advanced Nursing*, vol. 66, no. 10, 2010, pp. 2142-2153.

Gabbert, Tatjana I., et al. "Use of Social Networking Sites by Parents of very Low Birth Weight Infants: Experiences and the Potential of a Dedicated Site." *European Journal of Pediatrics*, vol. 172, no. 12, 2013, pp. 1671-1677.

Garthus-Niegel, Susan, et al. "The Impact of Subjective Birth Experiences on Post-Traumatic Stress Symptoms: A Longitudinal Study." *Archives of Women's Mental Health*, vol. 16, no. 1, 2013, pp. 1-10.

Goer, Henci, et al. "Vaginal or Caesarean Birth: What is at Stake for Women and Babies?" *Childbirth Connection*, National Partnership for Women and Families, 2012, childbirthconnection.org. Accessed 23 Nov. 2015.

Houston, Kathyrn, et al. "Mode of Delivery and Postpartum Depression: The Role of Patient Preferences." *American Journal of Obstetrics and Gynecology*, vol. 212, no. 2, 2015, pp. 229 e1-229.e7.

Lemola, Sakari, et al. "Maternal Adjustment Five Months After Birth: The Impact of the Subjective Experience of Childbirth and Emotional Support from the Partner." *Journal of Reproductive and Infant Psychology*, vol. 25, no. 3, 2007, pp. 190-202.

Lowe, Nancy K. "The Overuse of Caesarean Delivery." *Journal of Obstetric, Gynecologic, & Neonatal Nursing*, vol. 42, no. 2, 2013, pp. 135-136.

Magee, Susanna R., et al. "Promotion of Family-Centered Birth with Gentle Caesarean Delivery." *The Journal of the American Board of Family Medicine*, vol. 27, no.5, 2014, pp. 690-693.

McDaniel, Brandon T., et al. "New Mothers and Media Use: Associations between Blogging, Social Networking, and Maternal Wellbeing." *Maternal and Child Health Journal*, vol. 16, no. 7, 2012, pp. 1509-1517.

Moehler, E., et al. "Maternal Depressive Symptoms in the Postnatal Period are Associated with Long-Term Impairment of Mother-Child Bonding." *Archives of Women's Mental Health*, vol. 9, no. 5, 2006, pp. 273-278.

Niela-Vilen, H., et al. "Internet-Based Peer Support for Parents: A Systematic Integrative Review." *International Journal of Nursing Studies*, vol. 1, no. 11, 2014, pp. 1524-1537.

Olde, Eelco, et al. "Posttraumatic Stress Following Childbirth: A Review." *Clinical Psychology Review*, vol. 26, no.1, 2006, pp. 1-16.

Prior, Emily, et al. "Breastfeeding after Caesarean Delivery: A Systematic Review and Meta-analysis of World Literature." *The American Journal of Clinical Nutrition*, vol. 95, no. 5, 2012, pp. 1113-1135.

Shealy, Katherine R., et al. *The CDC Guide to Breastfeeding Interventions*. U.S. Department of Health and Human Services, Centers for Disease Control and Prevention, 2005.

Stadtlander, Lee. "The Impact of Current Trends in Caesarean Section." *International Journal of Childbirth Education*, vol. 29, no. 1, 2014, pp. 71.

Staub, Ervin, and Johanna Vollhardt. "Altruism Born of Suffering: The Roots of Caring and Helping After Victimization and Other Trauma." *American Journal of Orthopsychiatry*, vol. 78, no. 3, 2008, pp. 267-280.

Taffel, Selma M. et al. "Trends in the United States Caesarean Section Rate and Reasons for the 1980-85 Rise." *American Journal of Public Health*, vol. 77, no. 8, 1987, 955-959.

Taylor, Karen, et al. "Telling the Story, Hearing the Story: Narrative Co-Construction and Crisis Research." *American Communication Journal*, vol. 9, no. 1, 2007, ac-journal.org/journal/2007/Spring/articles/co-construction.html. Accessed 25 Aug. 2016.

Tedeschi, Richard G., et al. *Posttraumatic Growth: Positive Changes in the Aftermath of Crisis.* Lawrence Erlbaum Associates, 1998.

United States. United States Department of Health and Human Services. *The Surgeon General's Call to Action to Support Breastfeeding.* NCBI, 2011, www.ncbi.nlm.nih.gov/books/NBK52682/. Accessed 25 Aug. 2016.

World Health Organization (WHO). *Statement on Caesarean Section Rates. World Health Organization*, WHO, 2015, www.who.int/reproductivehealth/publications/maternal_perinatal_health/cs-statement/en/. Accessed 25 Aug. 2016.

7.
Mothering is NOT a Game

Game-Changing Measures for Parenting Education

AMY E. CROSS

When I became a mother at the age of twenty-eight, I lived far from family and friends who had experience in the realm of mothering. I had no experience. With every sneeze, I was convinced that my son had a life-threatening illness. Every cry was an indication of my failure to protect and keep healthy this little being who was suddenly thrust into my shaky arms. After nine months, I was not only a new mother but also a single mother. I was terrified. Fortunately, for both of us, my son's doctor recommended a parenting class. The only one running at the time was for parents of children five to twelve years of age. The toddler classes would be held a few months later. I decided to sign up for both.

The classes were offered through the state's Department of Health and Human Services offices, and most of the parents who were taking the class had been mandated by the state to attend. These parents were either in jeopardy of losing custody of their children to the state or had already lost custody and were attending with the sole mission of having their children returned. Many were fighting drug addictions or in domestic abuse situations. All of them were women, and all of them were on some sort of state assistance. My classmates all assumed that the same held true for me.

During the class breaks, we would huddle outside, smoke cigarettes, and talk about our situations as the smoke curled above our heads. I did not tell them that I was there of my own volition. I did not want them to feel as though I was passing judgment, and I wanted to belong. Looking back now, I wish that I had told them. Instead, I feel that I contributed to the stigma that comes with seeking parenting classes. Few of us are willing to admit that when it comes to mothering, we often do not know what we are doing. It should not be a stigma to say that we do not know how to be parents ... but it is.

Many years later, after taking two parenting classes and raising two healthy and happy boys, I constantly find myself returning to the information that I learned through those classes. I will never forget the first time that my son looked at me and screamed, "I hate you!" He was nearly three years old. We were in a grocery store, and he wanted something that I simply could not afford. My "No, honey, I'm sorry" response was not well received. He threw a tantrum and following the advice of the curriculum, I left the store, cart and all, and removed us both from the situation. He fought me all the way, screaming, "I hate you!" He finally stopped when I buckled him in his car seat, and he knew for sure that I was not going to change my mind. I then spoke gently to him, tilted my rearview mirror down to look in his red and steaming eyes, and said, "That's okay, honey. I'll just love you enough for both us." It worked, and it has worked every time since. Those classes have served me well as a mother, a youth mentor, and as a foster parent.

Unfortunately, many people believe that parent education addresses parenting issues from a "retrospective lens" rather than from a preventative perspective (Olabode et al. 21). This leads to an assumption—by the parents and towards the parents—that they are attending because of issues they have as opposed to seeking preventative tools. Others believe that family issues, such as parenting, should not be discussed outside of the home (Dempster et al. 2). The situation is made even more complicated by funding cuts to state programs and agencies that offer parenting classes.

A project in the state of Maine hopes to alleviate some of the issues around the accessibility of parenting classes and the stigma attached to attending those available ones. In this chapter, I analyze this pilot project and consider the potential advantages of using social media to conduct parenting classes in a virtual environment. I examine how the anonymity that the avatar provides in virtual reality environments may encourage more parents to participate in classes because such a social media mechanism allows mothers to avoid the real or perceived stigma attached to parenting classes.

The use of an avatar in such classes allows parents to participate more fully and comfortably, and provides the necessary instructor and peer contact.

MAINE PARENTS' PLACE PROJECT

In 2010, the Family Domain of the Maine Children's Growth Council outlined challenges to parenting education statewide in its white paper "Parenting Education in Maine." One of the challenges put forth was that "rural, sparsely populated areas present challenges to delivery" (Forstadt et al.). Because of the large rural population in Maine, parenting classes may not be readily accessible to parents desiring or required to take these classes. Many parents, even in places that offer these classes, may not have the transportation or the childcare resources necessary to facilitate their participation, and many others may not attend simply because of the stigma attached to attendance. Moreover, the funding for state programs in Health and Human Services has been dramatically cut across the state, which further complicates matters for parents in Maine.

The Family Domain put forth recommendations that included the identification of a "network(s) that will be the core delivery network of a core collection of evidence based primary/secondary parent education programming." This led to the formation of a project committee comprised of seven statewide agencies,[1] which determined that virtual world environments could provide comprehensive and consistent access to sorely needed parenting education programs (Forstadt et al.). For the purposes of this chapter, "a virtual world" is a computer-based, Internet 3D community environment shared by users interacting in a simulated world. Users interact with one another through text-based or voice-capable graphic models called avatars. Avatars are 3D images generated by a program into a virtual environment. Users can control their avatars using input devices, such as a keyboard, mouse, or other specially designed command and simulation gadgets. Virtual worlds are always available (persistent) and afford interactivity with other avatars and the environment itself. Some examples of virtual worlds include Second Life, World of Warcraft, and Minecraft.

The specific goals for the Maine Parent's Place Project, as the project came to be known, were threefold:

- Improve statewide access to parent education and other resources.
- Shorten wait times for parents who need to take parent education classes.
- Achieve cost savings, efficiency, and consistency in parent education in Maine (Forstadt et al.).

Over the next two years, the project committee was tasked with determining how to provide virtual parenting resources in a state ranking forty-ninth among the fifty states in Internet speed (Akamai 22) and only slightly higher than the national average in household computer ownership (Anderson) and Internet service access (File and Ryan 14).

Virtual parenting classes held in a synchronous manner were important to the project. Because many of the parents were mandated by the state to participate, it was important to make certain that their online training met the same standards as the face-to-face classes. Virtual classes must provide a comparable experience for the students. They also must provide a way for instructors to deliver information to the students and assess the students' learning.

The project committee developed the following student objectives for the pilot project:

- Learn new parenting skills, attitudes, and behaviours virtually.
- Easily set up avatars and navigate in the Maine Parent's
- Place virtual classroom using personal technology, the resources provided, and support from project staff.
- Actively participate in the virtual parent education classes.
- Easily see and hear what was being taught and discussed while in the Maine Parent's Place virtual classroom.
- Feel connected to other students and instructors while taking the classes.

For the project pilot, Maine Parent's Place collaborated with

Active Parenting Publishers to use Active Parenting Now Fourth Edition (APN), a six-part evidence-based course listed on SAMH-SA[2]'s National Registry of Evidence-Based Programs and Practices (NREPP). APN is widely used in Maine, and several project committee members are certified APN trainers. A video and discussion based program, Active Parenting was selected by the project committee, in part, because of its early integration of technology in parenting education.

Once the objectives were formed, the next challenge was to find technological expertise to evaluate and recommend technology platforms from which to deliver the classes, which is how I became involved with the project. As an interdisciplinary PhD student, my research centres around virtual technology and the effects of the avatar in learning environments. Virtual world environments are a mainstay for the new generation of learners. They acquire "stem" (science, technology, engineering, and math), design, critical thinking and problem-solving skills, often without realizing that such learning is occurring. They can create their own world and write scripts that animate objects or other avatars. They can also collaborate through the editing of objects in the virtual world. This technology is widely used in several education environments.

I had just completed my master's work, published my thesis, and was gaining recognition for my research in virtual technology when I was approached by Leslie Forstadt and Julie Della-Matterra—two of the authors of the "Parenting Education in Maine" white paper. They had heard of my work and attended one of my presentations on virtual technology uses in education at the University of Maine. I was subsequently introduced to the project coordinator for the Maine Parent's Place Project. Over the course of the next eighteen months, I worked with the team to evaluate several educational platforms, including virtual- and avatar-based platforms and web conferencing technologies that did not include avatars but provided a means to deliver the curriculum synchronously at a distance.

Based on our evaluations, we decided that Avaya's AvayaLive Engage, a web-browser-based virtual platform, provided the most robust environment with all of the technological requirements (analytics, voice and webcam, PowerPoint and video) and was easily accessible. Many virtual platforms require a software download and have above average graphic capabilities that require a steep learning curve. AvayaLive Engage is as simple as opening a Firefox or Safari browser, providing the web address for the virtual location, and downloading a plug-in to use it for the first time.

Virtual worlds such as AvayaLive Engage have provided a rich and robust research environment for many years. Several long-term studies and research projects have expounded the benefits of using this technology in educational and therapeutic applications, including a 2013 study conducted by Yoon and Vargas on "The Unintended Effect of Virtual-Self Representation on Behavior." They concluded that "[h]uman social responses can be altered by how virtual-self representations are implemented" (Yoon and Vargas 4).

A focus for the studies around psychological disorders and virtual learning involves Rotter's "locus of control," which is the extent to which individuals believe that their life circumstances are a function of either their own actions or external factors beyond their control (Lowes and Lin 19; Wallach et al. 30). Many studies have attested to the power of immersive virtual environments (IVEs) in influencing behaviour modification in several ways (Murray et al. 1350). The individual enters the virtual environment through a first-person perceptive—seeing, hearing, and reacting as though they were in the physical world. In a recent study by Stanford University, researchers put participants in one of two situations to gauge the effects of their experiences in an environmental situation. Some participants watched videos and read text-based websites on the environmental impact of paper production and usage. Other participants were immersed in a virtual environment that provided them with first-hand experience of actually cutting down a tree and experiencing the effects of this on a forested area. Those who participated in IVEs consumed 20 percent less paper than the participants who read websites and watched videos. IVE participants also "elicited greater self-reported internal environmental locus of control and self-reported environmental behaviors than print and video messages one week following the virtual experience" (Ahn et al. 235). By using IVEs, researchers were able to modify the behaviours of the participants through activities and situations designed around promoting healthy behaviours. By using high-tech graphics and embodied (avatar) experiences, these environments can provide users with the opportunity to practise realistic situations in a variety of settings, such as job interviews and, in our case, difficult parenting situations. These experiences are comparable to a "real world" role-play situation, and the effects on the user are the same as those experienced in the physical world.

SETTING UP THE STUDY

Four students referred by committee members and agency field staff participated in the pilot classes. Though no compensation was provided, participants received APN parent handbooks free of charge and were given a certificate of completion at the end of the six-class session. Targeted participants were rural parents, parents unable to attend physically because of childcare issues, and those that felt stigmatized in physical classes. All of the students were somewhat representative of the project's target audience:

•a single-parent mother based in Bangor, Maine, with a four-year-old child who had previously taken a traditional class and had felt uncomfortable;
•parents of a nine-year-old child, a husband and wife, thirty-two and twenty-eight respectively, based in Madison, Maine, a rural community; and
•a mother, thirty-four years old, based in Livermore Falls, with three children, ages twelve, ten, and eight, one of whom has special needs.

Prior to the classes, the project coordinator and I gave students a brief project orientation via the phone, a one-on-one orientation in the virtual classroom, and an Avaya user guide as a reference. I gave the instructors two practice sessions in the virtual classroom. The six-week classes were held in August and September 2015. All of the students and instructors were aware of their participation in a research study and were provided with informed consent documentation.

The data for this study was collected through survey monkey, an independent survey site that provides secure encryption tools to protect the identity of respondents. I asked participants eighteen questions regarding their experience as students using an avatar, their comfort in the virtual environment, and their feelings of connectedness with the other students and the instructor. I also included questions regarding obstacles and advantages that they experienced with the technology.

Active Parenting Now provided additional survey questions to the parent participants, which they answered prior to the start of classes and in the days following. Those questions were intended to assess the curriculum. Finally, the project coordinator conducted follow-up interviews with participants regarding their experience of the class, the curriculum, and the environment.

LOOKING AT THE RESULTS OF THE STUDY

Using the Survey Monkey site, all of the students reported that it was "easy" or "very easy" to access the virtual environment, navigate, hear, text, and chat in Maine Parent's Place. Similarly, when asked if anything prevented them from learning in Maine Parent's Place, all students answered "nothing" or "no." One student reported some discomfort in the virtual classroom during the first class; though by class six, all students reported feeling "very comfortable." Students were unanimous in feeling connected to their instructors despite participating as avatars for the entirety of the class. The anonymity provided by the virtual platform reportedly enhanced the students' experience. One student summed up the general feeling by noting that "no one can view you, so you feel comfortable asking questions openly."

We followed up by interviewing each of the students. Interview feedback from the students was overwhelmingly positive; all stated they would like to take more virtual parenting classes. We asked students in the first class about their experiences, and their responses were that it was "lively," and "pretty easy." One student offered that she liked the classroom set-up with posters linked to additional parenting information and that she had looked at them all. A third student admitted that she had some confusion in the beginning about the best way to communicate (via voice, text, etc.), but that this was resolved as the classes continued and teachers built a rapport among students.

We asked students in the final class for their impressions, and they responded that it was very "smooth," and that the material was well presented. One student appreciated the instructors' ability to "ad lib," in order to provide additional detail to make concepts more understandable.

When asked "What was difficult for you in this learning environment?" all students immediately responded that nothing was a deterrent, although one person noted that she sometimes had difficulty loading videos because of the limited Internet connectivity available in her rural town.

Finally, when asked "What was easy for you in this learning environment?" one student stated she preferred not having to drive to classes. Another said, "It was non-threatening and easy to participate. I can be affected in a negative way by people's body language in an in-person setting. Here, this wasn't a problem." One student admitted that although not a "tech person," and originally not "looking forward to the class," he was very satisfied and would take more virtual parenting classes in the future.

Active Parenting Now includes a student survey to gauge pre- and postclass parenting attitudes and beliefs, and provides an opportunity for course assessment. We also used this information to assess the students' experience with the virtual class. Three scales are used for this assessment. The Parent Attitudes and Beliefs scale addresses the parent's general attitudes and beliefs regarding a parent's responsibility to their children and vice versa. The Parent Observation of Child Behaviour scale focuses on their children's specific behaviours. Finally, the Parental Behaviours scale measures the parent's actions with their children. For all three scales, a higher overall score provides evidence of improved parenting understandings. Students were asked to complete and return the survey within a few weeks of class completion. For participants in the virtual world class, results showed an average increase of

•two points on the Parent Attitudes and Beliefs scale,

• four points on the Parent Observation of Child Behaviour scale, and
• seventeen points on the Parental Behaviours scale.

When compared to a random sample of APN students taught by the same instructor using the traditional in-person classroom delivery, the pilot students showed lower outcome scores on the "Parent Attitudes and Beliefs" scale (+7 vs. +2); the same outcome on the "Parent Observation of Child Behaviour" scale (+4); and higher scores on the "Parental Behaviours" scale (+17 compared to +7). In addition to the virtual nature of the pilot class, other factors differed with the face-to-face classes measured: the pilot was team taught and the traditional class was not; we used the fourth edition for the pilot while the traditional class used the third edition; and surveys were conducted one to two weeks post class during the pilot, but completed during the last class session at the in-person class. However, the results of the curriculum survey suggest that virtual delivery may positively modify behaviour more than in-person methods of instruction.

WHAT DID WE CONCLUDE?

Our student group was very small, and no major decisions regarding the long-term efficacy of virtual parenting classes can be made based on the results. However, the findings do provide a promising glimpse into the potential of virtual technology in the delivery of parenting classes. The participating parents, who are representative of the target group for the APN classes, were unanimously positive regarding their experience in the virtual classroom and, most importantly, they were able to incorporate some of the skills that they learned into their lives as parents. They also expressed interest in taking additional parenting classes through virtual technology.

Virtual education is a fast growing field; this project represents a groundbreaking innovation in parenting education that also addresses the unmet needs of communities, often in rural areas, who desire or are mandated to take parenting classes. For a variety of reasons, parents may not be able to participate in face-to-face parenting classes. Virtual classes provide a new opportunity to reach them. Additionally, virtual parenting classes may be more inviting to parents from small communities who worry about negative social consequences if they are seen in a class. This delivery method may also appeal to parent educators with limited travel budgets.

This small research study has provided both the Maine Parent's Place and this researcher with the opportunity to move the idea of virtual parenting classes to the next stage. My dissertation project will expand on the results of this study and will compare face-to-face delivery with a virtual class. The project will incorporate role-play into the classes and use real life participants in childlike scenarios in the physical class and virtual role-play with a child avatar in the virtual class. Through this study, I will further explore the effects that the anonymity of the avatar has on the parents' ease in the classroom, and how elements of the virtual world, including avatars, affect participants' thoughts and behaviours.

Perhaps, for some, mothering is an intuitive and innate proposition. It was not for me or for many others that I have known and have mentored. Parenting can be a struggle under the very best of conditions and a downright terrifying endeavour for those who struggle with addiction, poverty, or abuse. For those who are afraid or ashamed to reach out because of the stigmas attached to participating in a parenting class, virtual classes with an anonymous avatar may open up new avenues and opportunities. Having the support of an instructor and fellow classmates in a virtual domain allows parents to concentrate on the material and ask tough questions that may seem too embarrassing to ask in a face-to-face environment.

For me, parenting classes were life altering. They provided a set of tools that I continue to draw upon as I raise both my boys and interact with other children. Not all classes are created equally, and there is no one-size-fits-all solution in parenting education. In my experience, having the right tools in times of stress has given me the wherewithal to be a better mother. I do not know if I would have taken the classes back then had I fully understood the stigma attached to education in parenting or had I grown up in that community. I would like to think that I would have, but I cannot be sure. I can say without hesitation, however, that had the opportunity been there for me to attend virtual parenting classes from my living room, in my pajamas, I would most definitely have attended, and I would likely have asked more difficult questions than I felt comfortable asking in person.

I am the mother, the mentor, and the youth advocate that I am today in large part because of the parenting classes that I took nearly thirty years ago. Mothering in the twenty-first century may present mothers with different obstacles but as we move forward, I hope technology will provide us with some new tools with which to face those obstacles.

NOTES

[1]Agencies represented on the Maine Parent's Place Project Committee include Maine Children's Trust, Maine Department of Health and Human Services' Office of Child and Family Services and Office of Health Equity, University of Maine Cooperative Extension, University of Maine College of Education and Human Development, Maine Child Abuse and Neglect Councils, Strengthening Maine Families Program, Maine Families Home Visitation Program, and Touchpoints for Maine.

[2]SAMHSA is the Substance Abuse and Mental Health Services Administration and is a branch of the United States Department of Health and Human Services and leads public health efforts to advance the behavioral health of the nation.

WORKS CITED

Ahn, Sun Joo, et al. "Short- and Long-Term Effects of Embodied Experiences in Immersive Environments." *Computers in Human Behavior*, vol. 39, 2014, pp. 235-245.

Akamai Solutions, Content Delivery Provider Services. "State of the Internet Report" *Akamai*, Akamai, 2012, www.akamai.com/us/en/our-thinking/state-of-the-internet-report/. Accessed 15 Sept. 2015.

Anderson, J. Craig. "Maine Broadband Service Ranks 49th out of 50 States," *Portland Press Herald*, Maine Today Media, 8 Jan. 2014, http://www.pressherald.com/2014/01/08/maine_broadband_going_nowhere_fast__service_ranks_49th_out_of_50_states_/.

Accessed 15 Sept. 2015.

Dempster, Robert, et al. "The Role of Stigma in Parental Help-Seeking for Perceived Child Behavior Problems in Urban, Low-Income African American Parents". *Journal of Clinical Psychology in Medical Settings*, vol. 22, no. 4, 2015), pp. 265-278.

File, Thom and Camille Ryan. "Computer and Internet Use in the U.S., 2013." *American Community Survey Reports*, US Census Report, 2014, www.census.gov/history/pdf/2013computeruse.pdf. Accessed 20 Oct. 2015.

Forstadt L., et al. *Parenting Education in Maine: A White Paper for the Maine Children's Growth Council*. University of Maine, 2011.

Lowes, Susan and Peiyi Lin. "Learning to Learn Online: Using Locus of Control to Help Students Become Successful Online Learners". *Journal of Online Learning Research*, vol. 1, no. 1, 2015, pp. 17-48.

Murray, Craig D. et al. "Absorption, Dissociation, Locus of Control and Presence in Virtual Reality." *Computers in Human Behavior*, vol. 23, no. 3, 2007, pp. 1347-1354.

Olabode, Kristi, et al. "The State of Parent Education in Dallas County: Opportunities for the Future, Children at Risk Summary Report." *Childrenatrisk*. Children at Risk, 2014, http://173.45.238.175/content/wp-content/uploads/2014/12/NTX-Parent-education-needs-assessment-FINAL.pdf. Accessed 1 May 2016.

Wallach, Helene S. et al. "Personality Variables and Presence." *Virtual Reality*, vol. 14, no. 1, 2010, pp. 3-13. .

Yoon, Gunwoo and Patrick T. Vargas. "Know Thy Avatar: The Unintended Effect of Virtual-Self Representation on Behavior." *Psychological Science*, vol. 25, no. 4, 2014, pp. 1043-1045.

III.
MOTHERS, RESISTANCE, AND SOCIAL MEDIA

8.
From "Fakebooking" and "Flaming" to a "Mom's Support Network"

Reinforcing and Resisting Intensive Mothering Online

BRONWEN L. VALTCHANOV, DIANA C. PARRY AND
TROY D. GLOVER

T HE CULTURAL CONSTRUCTION OF MOTHERHOOD in the twenty-first century involves a powerful ideology of motherhood that shapes mothers' lived realities. Although a number of varied ideologies influence mothers, the current prevailing ideology of motherhood in North America is intensive mothering. It characterizes mothering as exclusive, entirely child centred, emotionally involving, and time consuming (Ennis; Hays). Within this ideology, mothers must "do it all" without complaint, and they must do it alone (Lloyd and Hawe). Moreover, the internalization of this ideology sets up a competition among women (Tardy) who scrutinize each other's behaviour according to the intensive mothering ideology (Oliver). In short, intensive mothering is a restrictive ideology of motherhood that compels mothers to conceal their lived realities, compete with other mothers, ignore their own needs, and focus entirely on their children.

Unsurprisingly, this ideology contributes to an anxiety-inducing culture of motherhood that leaves many mothers feeling inadequate (Warner), isolated (Drentea and Moren-Cross), and unsupported (Parry et al.). When mothers (inevitably) fall short of meeting the unrealistic expectations of intensive mothering, there are often significant consequences, including depression, decreased work-life balance, and negative feelings towards motherhood (Hilbrecht et al.; Oliver). Ultimately, intensive mothering instigates "the modern mother's need for continual perfection ... [which] cripples a mother's agency and confines her to a realm of mothering that is unattainable and unforgiving" (Oliver 19).

To cope with these challenges, mothers increasingly turn to the Internet as a source of community to connect, communicate, and share their experiences with other mothers (Drentea and Moren-Cross). Through internet technologies, including online communities and (SNSs), there is unprecedented interactivity among mothers. Currently, the majority of North American mothers regularly spend time online. For instance, in terms of SNSs specifically, almost 80 percent of American mothers use Facebook (Brenner and Smith), and nearly 60 percent of Canadian mothers visit SNSs daily (Canadian Digital Mom). Mothers' online interactivity has the potential to enable them to feel empowered and to resist intensive mothering by virtue of coming together to connect around shared interests, experiences, and identities (Moravec) and by forming friendships and receiving social support (Madge and O'Connor; Parry et al.; Valtchanov et al.). However, although contexts can provide an empowering virtual space in which mothers can individually and collectively resist intensive mothering, they also reinforce the ideology through mothers' enactments (Tuttle-Singer), including the expression of criticism and judgement of other mothers (Leavitt; Ley).

Thus, mothers transform their social context through online connections, which present new forms of interactions with intensive mothering. To explore the experiences and implications of mothers' online connections and interactions with intensive mothering, we embarked on a research project with *momstown.ca*—a Canadian social networking site that facilitates an online community and connects mothers both in cyberspace and face to face.

STUDY OVERVIEW

Momstown.ca (hereafter called Momstown) began in 2007 as a unique entrepreneurial endeavour combining both geographical and online community building for mothers. It provides both online and face-to-face services specifically based in local communities across Canada.[1] Momstown's primary online service involves a discussion forum and message board, which enables women to meet online, chat with one another, seek and offer advice, and if necessary, vent. For an annual membership fee of forty-five dollars, mothers and their families also access an online calendar that schedules over twenty monthly events in the local community, including events exclusively for mothers (e.g., Moms' Night Out) as well as events for both mothers and their children (from birth until six years of age).

This research involved active interviews with twenty-two Momstown members from one Southern Ontario chapter. This particular chapter was representative of many Momstown chapters, both in terms of the size of the city in which it is based and the size of the membership. Within this chapter, participant recruitment techniques included an email advertisement sent to each member of the chapter through an "e-blast"—an invitational post on the Momstown message board—and a brief talk given at an organized Momstown event. We also used snowball sampling to recruit participants (Patton); at the end of each interview, participants were asked to suggest other members of Momstown who were willing to participate in this study. Through these methods, we recruited twenty-two participants (identified pseudonymously in the findings). In the interviews, we asked participants to discuss their experiences of motherhood, Momstown, and other online contexts for mothers. As such, our research reflects several online contexts, including Momstown, Facebook, and a variety of local and national online motherhood forums (for a more detailed discussion of the study's methodology, see Parry et al.).

Our study was guided by the theoretical framework of "cyberfeminism," which focuses on the relationship between gender and digital culture through an examination of women's engagement with internet technologies (Flanagan and Booth). Cyberfeminism is a particularly relevant theoretical approach for our study given its acknowledgement and elucidation of how women's Internet practices affect their lives in "complex ways that both resist and reinforce hierarchies of gender" (Daniels 101). We turn now to our findings, which reflect the complexities of mothers' experiences online as they encounter both the reinforcement and resistance of intensive mothering.

FINDINGS

Reinforcement of Intensive Mothering Online
Mothers' engagement with online environments transform their

interactions with other mothers and subsequently, with the reinforcement of intensive mothering. A number of mothers in this study lament some mothers' use of Facebook to publicly project the image of the supermom. Although these mothers use the term "supermom," they do not identify supermotherhood as a form of intensive mothering by specifying this less colloquial term. They do, however, recognize that supermotherhood is indeed an image that mothers construct and project. Heather remarks: "I have one person on Facebook and her statuses are always like, 'Up at 5:00 a.m., I made muffins and cleaned the house.' [She is] excited about everything. The one day, her [status] was like, 'We got up at 3:00 a.m., so me and [my daughter] hung out.'" This mother's Facebook projections emphasize "do[ing] it all" and doing so without complaint. These virtual projections reproduce the selflessness and child-centred insistences of intensive mothering.

These same characteristics of intensive mothering are emphasized when mothers criticize and judge other mothers for not practicing intensive mothering. As Elizabeth comments, this occurred on Facebook as she reached out for support but instead received harsh judgment:

> I was sleep training [my daughter] at night 'cause I just could not get up seven times a night anymore, and she was a year old. She was in that full on scream bloody murder for two hours, so I'm sitting there at the top of the stairs, and I put [on Facebook], "Okay moms, how do you handle this?" Forty-five comments later, during the screaming, three-quarters of them told me I was doing child abuse.

In addition to mothers' negative experiences on Facebook, they also encounter the reinforcement of intensive mothering on a number of online forums for mothers. In particular, mothers describe pervasive judgment and unsolicited advice about their choices as mothers, which underscore intensive mothering's narrow conception of a "good" mother. Bethany relates the following:

> [Posts] can get catty sometimes. One girl posted about having difficulty breastfeeding and what kind of bottle

should she go to for formula. And so many people posted saying, "Do you absolutely have to do formula?" "Maybe you should try pumping and then feeding him out of a cup or spoon-feeding or using a syringe." And I'm [thinking] like, "She wants to use a bottle, she didn't ask you for your [advice on] whether she should stop [breast]feeding." It does feel judgey. [There is] absolutely nothing like it. Like, high school hazing and trying to fit in and all that stuff, that's compared [to the judgment of mothers].

Bethany's observation of the judgmental attitudes on many online forums for mothers speaks to the irony of mothers seeking community, only to find exclusion. This same irony is demonstrated for Elizabeth, above, who seeks support but receives judgement. These experiences highlight how mothers can seek out support and community online only to encounter the very judgement and exclusion that they encounter offline and are seeking to avoid.

The attitudes and values of users within online spaces for mothers are often expressed in discussions of "hot topics," which are polarizing or controversial. Katherine explains her reluctance to participate in online discussions or posts about such topics: "Sometimes, I would refrain from posting on [the] Baby Bells [forum] 'cause I thought, 'Oh somebody's going to jump down my throat about that.' You learn real quick [the] things you never talk about at a baby playgroup [or online]—unless you want to start a fight—are vaccines, breastfeeding, and circumcision." Bethany echoes this "common" negativity online in asserting, "If somebody posts something, they get a flood of people telling them why they shouldn't do something that way. 'Cause that's common online, people saying, 'This is the way to do it, what you're doing is totally awful and you shouldn't do that at all.'" These judgmental online experiences reinforce intensive mothering by promoting narrow and rigid conceptions of "good" motherhood and an environment in which mothers do not feel free to openly discuss different approaches to mothering.

Some mothers resist judgement that they face. This is evident, for instance, in Bethany's response to the negativity that she identifies on a motherhood message board:

I started a thread a few months ago, which ended up being super controversial. I had just noticed that people would automatically jump in and say [unsolicited advice]. So I posted saying, "Has anybody noticed kind of a negative feel to the forum?" and it got so heated that one of the moderators pretty much reamed me out. I thought maybe we could agree that there has been a bit of negativity trending and maybe we could try to be more positive and supportive instead of automatically dumping on the [poster]. But, it ended up [getting] shut down by [a moderator]. People got so mad! They wanted me to point fingers to specific threads where there was negativity and I was like, "Look, I don't want to do that because it's not about individual people." [They said,] "This isn't half as bad as most forums online." I'm like, "It's a radical idea, [but] we can all be adults here."

This description further highlights another significant factor that influences mothers' experiences of online environments: the role of moderators. As Bethany relays, the moderator of this online forum reinforces intensive mothering and perpetuates its negativity by chastising her and shutting down her attempts to identify and improve the "negative feel" of the forum. Specifically, it is not negativity itself that necessarily reinforces intensive mothering, since "negativity" is a broad and often subjective term. For some, for instance, negativity may be any degree of critique or controversy. In this context, negativity does not refer to the topics being discussed but rather to the ways in which they are discussed: mothers who "jump in" with unsolicited and unsupportive advice or comments. This negative way of discussing topics online is a way of "dumping on" mothers, which reinforces the divisiveness and competition between them.

Surprisingly, improving this online negativity may be actively resisted by forum participants, including moderators, which suggests that expectations of mothers' online behaviour on many motherhood forums exist within a disappointing spectrum of "totally awful" to not "as bad." When the limiting intensive mothering ideology is reinforced online, mothers' individual parenting choices are undermined, their lived realities are concealed, and their potentially supportive connections to one another are jeopardized.

Resistance to Intensive Mothering Online

Amid online environments for mothers that often reinforce intensive mothering, the unique online and face-to-face community of Momstown provides a much-needed alternative. Several mothers compare their positive experiences with Momstown to their more negative experiences with Facebook. For instance, Julia emphasizes how Momstown's online community counters the "image" of intensive mothering: "I don't think people go [to Momstown] to put up an image. People go there because they're saying I need support, or I need to talk, or I need to hang out. [It's not] where people were to show off, [like, I] find a lot of liars on Facebook."

When mothers connect through authentic interactions rather than being divided through competition (or the need to "show off"), they foster openness and support that resists the demanding and isolating ideology of intensive mothering. As discussed above, one example of this ideology circulating on Facebook involves the "excited" mother who is eager to clean the house, make muffins, and entertain her daughter—all before dawn. Although this Facebook projection of supermotherhood serves to reinforce it, a mother's critical response to such projections can resist the ideology, even through the reader's own private mental response. Instead of simply accepting the all-too-common projection of supermotherhood that she encounters on Facebook, Heather's critical response is a suggestion for an alternative Facebook status, which cleverly subverts intensive mothering by rejecting the entirely child-centred approach: "I love being a mom, but it's not an easy job. If my kid gets up at 3:00 a.m., they are going back to bed; I don't care what they want to do. I'd be, 'Sent them back to bed, did not clean my house or make muffins. Now I'm having a nap.'"

The need to feel support rather than judgment is a crucial distinction emphasized in Elizabeth's discussion of the negativity that she experiences when sharing her sleep-training frustrations on Facebook (described above), in comparison to the "supportive dialogue" she encounters on her local Momstown message boards:

Here I am on Facebook, I was like, "What is this?!" And if I hadn't experienced seeing positive dialogues on our [Momstown message] boards before, I probably would have stopped [sleep training]. [But,] I know I could have gone to my local Momstown [message boards] and I would have gotten a whole bunch of moms saying, like, "Hang in there, go have a shower, go for a walk." People can have supportive dialogue.

Mothers also share their positive experiences on Momstown in contrast to a number of other online contexts beyond Facebook. Bethany explains how these positive online experiences facilitate the development of friendships: "I found Momstown conversations seem nicer [than other forums]. They seem very friendly and respectful and more socially appropriate. I was like, 'This is awesome!' 'cause we [moms] do get judging. It's really important that you are nice and respectful, especially up front, because that allows you to start a friendship with someone."

The attitude of respect on Momstown is further demonstrated within the context of "hot topics" in motherhood. As Elizabeth asserts, "We can discuss serious topics, like circumcision and breastfeeding and VBACS [vaginal birth after Caesarean section], or things that you think could be really hot, and they still are; there's debates. But, they're done [respectfully] versus these anonymous things where people scream at each other." Megan similarly shares, "We have all kinds of discussions [on the] discussion boards [and] people will be very opinionated about something, but it's never in a way of, 'Oh, well I think all moms who do this are crazy and are stupid and shouldn't do that.' It's not in a bashing other moms [way]."

These respectful exchanges on Momstown result from an awareness of the diverse approaches to mothering, which resists the ideological parameters of intensive mothering. As Alicia contends, "Everybody parents differently, so it's nice to see [on the Momstown forum] that there's all different ways to think and to parent and your way isn't necessarily the right way or the wrong way; it's just a way." This significant form of resistance to intensive mothering manifests itself in a simple yet powerful phrase that mothers on

Momstown see repeated often: "What works for me doesn't need to work for you."

One of the factors mothers discuss as facilitating Momstown's positive online environment is conscientious moderators. Bethany describes the overall role that online moderators play: "I think it's really important that the moderators set the tone. Like, with [the local] Momstown [owner-moderator], she was a very personable, friendly, optimistic type person." As Victoria adds, "I think because the Momstown [forums] are fairly closely moderated, a lot of that [negative] stuff doesn't surface on there." Thus, moderators can ensure a positive online environment by setting a respectful and friendly tone and by closely monitoring the forums to prevent or remove negative content.

Mothers also attribute the respectful environment to the annual membership fee Momstown members pay to participate in both the online forums and in-person events. This fee acts as a filter to discourage online posters simply looking to provoke "drama." As Bethany explains: "The [fee] keeps it to people who are really interested in the events and participating, versus people who just want a venue to spout what they think; for people who just want drama. Nobody's going to pay to go on there and say [something provocative] just to see what the reaction is 'cause you can do that for free on like three million other [forums]." In this way, the membership fee creates a significant distinction between Momstown and other online motherhood forums. Mothers who are truly invested in contributing to a community of mothers can demonstrate this investment by paying the membership fee. However, mothers who may be more interested in having an online venue to circulate their opinions and to see the reactions of others are unlikely to pay to do so when there are ample free forums.

Although conscientious moderators and a membership fee are important factors enabling the respectful and supportive experiences on Momstown, the lack of anonymity is perceived as particularly important in promoting a positive online environment. This results from Momstown's unique dual focus on regular face-to-face events and online forums, which means that members get to know one another both in-person and online. In Elizabeth's words:

I believe what makes us have the more welcoming, positive vibe that maybe other online communities don't have is that it's not anonymous. Like, on some anonymous online forums, people say things that there's no way they would ever say to your face. But, if [I] know I'm going to see them the next week, I might frame my comment a little nicer because I'm going to have to sit next to you at Moms' Night Out and I'd feel like a really big heel if I just told you [something] mean [online].

This online and in-person dynamic translates into accountability for online behaviour. As Victoria observes, "I think with Momstown, you don't get as much of that [negativity] because there is almost like a responsibility. You're held accountable for your words because you're going to meet that person on Saturday at wherever [event], so I think people are a little more cautious with what they say and what they post."

Ultimately, Momstown is a distinctly supportive environment. As Blair aptly describes, "[Momstown] is different. I really do think it's because we're neighbours. If you ask for advice, people will tell you, 'Well, this is what worked for me, or here's a really great resource for you, or try this and hope this works.' It's really very, very supportive." This support is essential for mothers and crucially resists the demand of intensive mothering that mothers should "do it alone." As Bethany insists, "Support [is] definitely important. I mean, you would just be almost on your own if you didn't have your moms' support network that you trust [and] it's nice to have that option online." This supportive online community of mothers fosters empowerment by challenging the pervasive, negative feelings of mothers who fall short of the expectations inherent to intensive mothering. As Julia concludes, "If you're feeling down, you're not going to feel empowered, so first has to come a positive feeling of being a mom. Then, from that comes, 'Okay, I can do this; I'm empowered to be a good mom.'" Momstown's distinctly positive online environment offers possibilities for a new cultural construction of motherhood that resists mothers' competition, judgement, and divisiveness and instead promotes friendliness, respect, and support among mothers.

DISCUSSION

Reinforcement of Intensive Mothering Online

The current construction of motherhood—conveyed by the powerful ideology of intensive mothering—results in stultifying and destructive consequences that leave many mothers feeling overwhelmed and inadequate (Warner). These consequences not only affect how women feel about themselves, but they also significantly affect women's connections to other women, as the competition promoted by intensive mothering "pits women against each other rather than join[ing] them against the structures that have created the idealization" (Tardy 440). This competition plays out in mothers' online spaces, as evidenced by the mothers in our study who share their resentment that some mothers "put up an image" by crafting narrative displays of intensive mothering. In particular, mothers experience the reinforcement of intensive mothering online in two distinct but related ways: first, through some mothers' described enactments of this ideology; and second, through online judgements levelled at mothers who are not behaving according to this ideology.

Participants in this study suggest that a primary way intensive mothering is reinforced in social media—through mothers' online enactments—is via Facebook. This is exemplified, for instance, with one mother conveying in her Facebook status that she is "excited about everything," including entertaining her daughter at 3:00 a.m., making muffins, and cleaning the house. Acknowledging the disparity between mothers' "real life" and the "airbrushed image" that many mothers present on Facebook, Sarah Tuttle-Singer coined the term "Fakebook." She asserts that this contemporary Fakebook phenomenon compels mothers to carefully stylize their posts and images in ways that "pretend" the challenges of motherhood do not exist, and in doing so publicly, mothers are "making friends on Facebook feel like they have to pretend as well" (107) in a reciprocal loop that reinforces intensive mothering.

Mothers experience the second way intensive mothering is reinforced online by being harshly judged when they express a consideration of their own needs and well-being, which challenges the selflessness and child-centred demands of intensive mothering

(Ennis; Hays). This is especially evident with "hot topic" issues in motherhood (Leavitt). Mothers in our study feel overtly judged for various parenting decisions or even for efforts to seek feedback on different approaches. They protest that it is "common online" for mothers to receive comments from other mothers conveying the message that "what you're doing is totally awful and you shouldn't do that at all," or to see discussion forums "where people scream at each other" over controversial topics in motherhood. These experiences are consistent with the online practice of "flaming"—directing rude or disparaging comments to an individual—which typically occurs within online environments in which users are engaged in contentious exchanges of opinion (Herring). Mothers' observation that this hostile online behaviour occurs because the relative anonymity of most sites is also consistent with broader research on computer-mediated communication that shows flaming pervades when there is low social accountability (Herring).

While mothers' experiences of flaming are congruent with other online environments—in terms of contentious topics and low social accountability from anonymity—the occurrence of flaming between mothers, and certainly its pervasiveness, defies gender patterns of communication that frequently occur online. Specifically, research on Internet spaces documenting gendered differences in online communication styles finds that females tend to use more supportive language, express appreciation more directly, and foster community building, whereas males generally use more confrontational language, self-promotion over community building, and the antagonistic practice of flaming (Chisholm). Thus, our finding of mothers' negative experiences of SNSs and online communities (other than Momstown) notably contrasts with research contending that flaming is a less common practice in women's online discussion groups (Sharf). In this sense, mothers' experiences of the competitive imperative of intensive mothering may in fact overturn the "genderscript" of traditionally female-oriented values (Ley) in favour of the confrontational, self-promotional, and antagonistic communication styles heretofore associated with males in online environments (Chisholm). This overturning of traditional gender expectations online may be attributed to two potential factors, working individually or collectively. First, the anonymity offered by many online environments may result in a neutralization of gender expectations, which was a central argument for cyberspace's potential for gender equality advanced by earlier forms of cyberfeminism (Fernandez et al.). Second, the cultural acceptability (and promotion) of intensive mothering as the current, dominant ideology of motherhood may give mothers permission to defy traditional gender expectations of femininity, generally, in order to uphold the particular gender expectations of motherhood, which currently include the *intensity* of intensive mothering with its competitive imperative. Notably, outside the context of intensive motherhood, a competitive imperative would typically be associated with males (Chisholm). Clearly, however, these hostile and judgmental interactions do not serve either gender and certainly do not benefit mothers.

Lastly, mothers in our study experience the reinforcement of intensive mothering through other mothers' overt resistance to identifying or changing the "negativity trending" within online motherhood message boards. This reinforcement—or resistance to resistance—is enacted by certain forum members and moderators. Understanding how this reinforcement operates (and possibilities for challenging it) must be situated within the social structures of online communities. In her discussion of computer-mediated discourse, Susan Herring reminds us that online communities, like all societal institutions, create social structures that "generate rules, sanctions against the violation of those rules, and systems of governance to enforce the sanctions, headed by empowered individuals or groups" (624). As mothers describe for many online motherhood communities, the "rules" allow for negativity, such as flaming. Mothers who try to challenge this are sanctioned by being "reamed out" or having their discussion posts "shut down" (i.e., removed) by empowered individuals, such as forum moderators or by groups, including the group of mothers on one forum who insist that their forum is not "half as bad" as other forums. This persistence of mothers' judgements towards other mothers warrants a consideration of what function it may serve for those who perpetuate this behaviour. Mothers who have become adept at projecting their (apparent) adherence to intensive mothering may view their projections—and their defense of these projections through judging others who are not practising them—as a way to boost self-esteem or to otherwise receive praise or validation from other mothers.

Furthermore, this defense of intensive mothering may extend to contentions that it may actually be the experience of some mothers rather than a projection or concealment of mothers' lived reality. Although it is important not to discredit any mother's sense of her own experiences on a broader ideological level rather than an individual level, suggesting that intensive mothering is an accurate framework for most mothers' realities is similar to suggesting that perfection itself is both realistic and attainable. Intensive mothering demands a kind of "continual perfection" in motherhood that is neither realistic nor attainable (Oliver 19). Thus, although there may appear to be short-term benefits to mothers' projections and defense of intensive mothering, reinforcing this ideology is detrimental to individual mothers and to mothers more broadly because it conveys expectations that are unrealistic, unhealthy, and unsustainable (Oliver). Even though mothers' experiences online reflect a context in which intensive mothering is reinforced, this context can also facilitate new ways of resisting this narrow ideology and its effects.

Resistance to Intensive Mothering Online

The often negative experiences many mothers encounter online provide a distinct comparison to mothers' positive experiences with a particular online community of mothers—Momstown. As such, Momstown offers a valuable context in which to examine how an online environment for mothers can foster supportive community building and resist the limiting ideology of intensive mothering, which can contribute to empowered mothering (O'Reilly).

Cyberfeminism's central recognition of the Internet's potential for women's positive transformation begins with individual women connecting to a community of women online (Daniels). However, simply connecting with other women online does not necessarily lead to feminist outcomes, and it may in fact impede them, such as when intensive mothering is enacted and enforced. (Cyber)feminist outcomes do become possible, however, when women feel a sense of community and support online, as the mothers in our study overwhelmingly report of their experiences with Momstown (Mulcahy et al.; Parry et al.; Valtchanov et al.). With this sense of community and support, mothers can develop connections rooted in authenticity because they do not feel judged (Ley). This environment of support and nonjudgement is uniquely facilitated within Momstown's online community because it connects mothers online who also connect face-to-face through regular events in the community, which makes Momstown both local and familiar. This spirit of acceptance is in sharp contrast with mothers' negative experiences with larger or more anonymous online environments, where "people say things that there's no way they would ever say to your face." Momstown's operation as a chapter-specific, geographically based online, and face-to-face group of local "neighbourhood moms" means that mothers are "held accountable for [their] words." This high social accountability virtually eliminates the flaming that occurs elsewhere online where low social accountability persists (Herring).

This supportive environment is maintained through what Herring refers to as the "*norms* of practice regarding 'how things are done' and what constitutes socially desirable behavior" (622). Momstown's norms are maintained through the effective combination of high social accountability, a membership fee (which discourages "drama"), close moderation (by "friendly" moderators), and members' ongoing observations of (and benefits from) a supportive online culture. Through these means, the Momstown online community compels socially desirable behaviour that members repeatedly describe as "friendly," "nice," "respectful," and "supportive." All of these behaviours resist the disparaging, competitive, judgmental, and alienating behaviours promoted by intensive mothering.

Within this supportive online community, openness and honesty translate into some mothers' desire to counter the messages perpetuated by intensive mothering in other online spaces. In this sense, they find the confidence required to advance the project of resistance and real social change. For instance, one mother responds to Tuttle-Singer's call for mothers to resist Fakebook by suggesting an alternative Facebook status update to the one that she observes from the "excited" mother. Her tongue-in-cheek comment parodies the absurdity of intensive mothering and emphasizes her own needs, which gives herself and other mothers permission to "stop pretending" (Tuttle-Singer 107).

Finally, mothers are able to resist intensive mothering online through the broad range of mothering experiences that they access, specifically within an online culture of support and nonjudgement. This supported breadth of experiences speaks to another key recognition of cyberfeminism's transformative potential as a communicative and participatory culture (Daniels). Within the culture of Momstown, mothers receive advice and information on mothering with the understanding that what works for one mother does not need to work for all mothers. In this way, mothers are exposed to a diversity of parenting approaches, which undermines intensive mothering's narrow conception of the "good mother." Women sharing their experiences online is a political act. Together, these women represent a virtual consciousness-raising group: "there is a feminist impulse in these mothers' desire to tell the truth about their life—a belief that simple honesty can perhaps change the outdated and impossible ideals of motherhood" (Jesella 32). Ultimately, in the face of an often hostile and isolating culture of motherhood—reinforced by such online realities as Fakebooking and flaming—the mothers in our study found an online "moms' support network" that bolsters their efforts to be empowered mothers on their own terms.

Acknowledgements: This research was funded by the Canadian Social Sciences and Humanities Research Council. The authors would like to thank the mothers who participated in the study for generously providing their time and insights. We would also like to thank the co-editors of this book for their thoughtful comments. Lastly, the first author would like to sincerely thank her two co-authors for encouraging and supporting her involvement in this important work.

NOTE

[1]When research interviews were conducted in the spring of 2011, Momstown operated as described in the chapter: a unique online

and face-to-face locally-based community of Canadian mothers. At the time, there were eighteen chapters across Canada and a one-year membership costs forty-five dollars. Since that time, the number of chapters expanded to twenty-four locations and the annual membership became a "program pass," which costs eighty-five dollars, to reflect the increased focus on early childhood development programs. More recently, in the fall of 2015, Momstown changed ownership and become an online-only resource, which is still dedicated to helping Canadian moms find information and support. As indicated on their website (still *momstown.ca*), the current Momstown is a "trusted, digital resource featuring a variety of content from parenting tips to family-friendly recipes to contest promotions." There is still a national Momstown website as well as individual websites for each of the now twenty Canadian cities that offer local content. Notably, the current Momstown is significantly different from the Momstown that was studied and that is discussed in this chapter in that it no longer has these features: face-to-face local events, an online members' message board, a membership fee, or chapters that are owned and operated by local mothers. Despite these changes to Momstown, this study remains relevant in providing insights on the characteristics of online motherhood forums that promote a supportive online community: combining face-to-face and virtual connections, which ensures high social accountability; a membership fee; close moderation of message boards; and members' commitment to a respectful online culture. An awareness of these characteristics is useful for both mothers and online forum developers. For mothers who are seeking a supportive online community, they are encouraged to look for motherhood forums with some or all of these characteristics. For the developers of the growing number of online motherhood forums, incorporating these characteristics can foster the kind of online environment in which mothers want to participate.

WORKS CITED

Brenner, Joanna, and Aaron Smith. "Wishing Mom a Happy Mother's Day ... on Facebook." *Pew Internet & American Life Project*, Pew Research Center, 8 May 2013, www.pewresearch.

org/fact-tank/2013/05/08/wishing-mom-a-happy-mothers-day-on-facebook/. Accessed 1 May 2015.

Canadian Digital Mom. *Canadian Digital Mom 2012 Report.* Mom Central Consulting, December 2012.

Chisholm, June F. "Cyberspace Violence Against Girls and Adolescent Females." *Annals of the New York Academy of Sciences,* vol. 1087, no. 1, 2006, pp. 74-89.

Daniels, Jessie. "Rethinking Cyberfeminism(s): Race, Gender, and Embodiment." *WSQ: Women's Studies Quarterly,* vol. 37, no. 1, 2009, pp. 101-124.

Drentea, Patricia, and Jennifer L. Moren-Cross. "Social Capital and Social Support on the Web: The Case of an Internet Mother Site." *Sociology of Health & Illness,* vol. 27, no. 7, 2005, pp. 920-943.

Ennis, Linda Rose, ed. *Intensive Mothering: The Cultural Contradictions of Modern Motherhood.* Demeter Press, 2014.

Fernandez, Maria, Faith Wilding, and Michelle M. Wright, editors. *Domain Errors!: Cyberfeminist Practices.* Autonomedia, 2002.

Flanagan, Mary, and Austin Booth. *Reload: Rethinking Women + Cyberculture.* MIT Press, 2002.

Hays, Sharon. *The Cultural Contradictions of Motherhood.* Yale University Press, 1996.

Herring, Susan C. "Computer-Mediated Discourse." *The Handbook of Discourse Analysis,* edited by Deborah Schiffrin, Deborah Tannen, and Heidi E. Hamilton, Blackwell Publishing, 2003, pp. 612-634.

Hilbrecht, Margo, et al. "'I'm Home for the Kids': Contradictory Implications for Work-Life Balance of Teleworking Mothers." *Gender, Work & Organization,* vol. 15, no. 5, 2008, pp. 454-476.

Jesella, Kara. "Naughty Mommies." *The American Prospect,* 20 March 2009, http://prospect.org/article/naughty-mommies. Accessed 26 Aug. 2016.

Leavitt, Sarah. "Threads of Dissent: Conflict in an Online Community." *Motherhood Online,* edited by Michelle Moravec, Cambridge Scholars Publishing, 2011, pp. 60-72.

Ley, Barbara L. "Vive les Roses!: The Architecture of Commitment in an Online Pregnancy and Mothering Group." *Journal of Computer-Mediated Communication*, vol. 12, no. 4, 2007, pp. 1388-1408.

Lloyd, Beverley, and Penelope Hawe. "Solutions Forgone? How Health Professionals Frame the Problem of Postnatal Depression." *Social Science & Medicine*, vol. 57, no. 10, 2003, pp. 1783-1795.

Madge, Clare, and Henrietta O'Connor. "Parenting Gone Wired: Empowerment of New Mothers on the Internet?" *Social & Cultural Geography*, vol. 7, no. 2, 2006, pp. 199-220.

Moravec, Michelle, editor. *Motherhood Online*. Cambridge Scholars Publishing, 2011.

Mulcahy, Caitlin M. "From Mothering Without a Net to Mothering on the Net: The Impact of an Online Social Networking Site on Experiences of Postpartum Depression." *Journal of the Motherhood Initiative for Research and Community Involvement*, vol. 6, no. 1, 2015, pp. 92-106.

Oliver, Nicole L. "The Supermom Syndrome: An Intervention Against the Need to Be King of the Mothering Mountain." master's thesis, Royal Roads University, 2011.

O'Reilly, Andrea, ed. *Feminist Mothering*. Albany: SUNY Press, 2008.

Parry, Diana C. et al. "From "Stroller-Stalker" to "Momancer": Courting Friends through a Social Networking Site for Mothers." *Journal of Leisure Research*, vol. 45, no. 1, 2013, pp. 22-45.

Patton, Michael Q. *Qualitative Research and Evaluation*. Sage, 2002.

Sharf, Barbara F. "Communicating Breast Cancer On-Line: Support and Empowerment on the Internet." *Women & Health*, vol. 26, no. 1, 1997, pp. 65-84. P

Tardy, Rebecca W. ""But I Am a Good Mom" The Social Construction of Motherhood through Health-Care Conversations." *Journal of Contemporary Ethnography*, vol. 29, no. 4, 2000, pp. 433-473.

Tuttle-Singer, Sarah E. "No More Fakebook." *The Good Mother Myth: Redefining Motherhood to Fit Reality*, edited by Avital Norman Nathman, Seal Press, 2014, pp. 107-112.

Valtchanov, Bronwen L., et al. "Neighborhood at your Fingertips:

Transforming Community Online through a Canadian Social Networking Site for Mothers." *Gender, Technology and Development*, vol. 18, no. 2, 2014, pp. 187-217.

Warner, Judith. *Perfect Madness: Motherhood in the Age of Anxiety.* Riverhead Books, 2005.

9.

Hip Mama

Mother Outlaws in Cyberspaces

ANITRA GORISS-HUNTER

Becoming a mother is cataclysmic. It is experienced in a myriad of ways but always the act signals change. As an academic, I turned to words, thoughts, and ideas to help me understand what I felt to be a complete and sometimes terrifying transformation of maternity. I found a copy of Adrienne Rich's *Of Woman Born* and read it. Rich's descriptions of the joys of mothering as well as her honest and critical insights into the institution of motherhood spoke about her journey into maternity. She was also speaking parts of *my* story of mothering. At the time that I discovered Rich's maternal writings, I had completed a project on the "bold new territory" of cyberspace. Having enjoyed the fiery feminism of the geekgirls, grrrls, and other activists as well as being excited by Rich's work, I turned to cyberspace, hungry for stories of mothering. What I found intriguing in this domain was the comingling of convention and subversion, and the enormous possibility for change. In the hope of finding representations of maternal bodies going beyond the normative images, I looked to an investigation of the cyber-realm and the potential of this domain to overturn dominant discourses of motherhood.

Searching for an alternative to the representations of the "good mother" that abound throughout commercial mothering websites, I turned to *Hip Mama*, a website for mothers interested in critical discussions and activism concerning a variety of political, artistic, and childrearing issues. The hip mamas comprise an online maternity community that is an alternative to the plethora of apolitical and commercial motherhood sites that abound throughout the

Internet. I contend that *Hip Mama* extends Andrea O'Reilly's notion of "mother outlaw" (*Mother Outlaws*; *From Motherhood to Mothering*; *Feminist Mothering*) into cyber(cultural)space. The latter term extends the popular notion of cyberspace as websites and online texts to include the concept of the cyber-domain as story, culture and experience. With David Bell (2), I argue that cyber(cultural)space is, foremost, "lived culture": the everyday interactions of people, technology, and story in cyber-realms.

The term "mother outlaw" refers to O'Reilly's reinvigoration of the conversation formally begun by Adrienne Rich in 1976 concerning the marking of a distinction between motherhood as institution and mothering as lived experience. O'Reilly argues that in order to embrace a feminist maternity of empowerment, maternal bodies need to reject the institution of motherhood and its stereotype of the good mother and turn to her opposite, the mother outlaw. This maternal outlaw figure refuses the culturally entrenched imperatives that demand mothers must be perpetually available and completely centred on domesticity and children.

In this chapter, I examine the ways in which the narratives of hip maternity intersect with and diverge from the consumption-driven maternal of the commercial mothering websites. First, I draw on the theories of Howard Rheingold and David Bell to interrogate the limits and boundaries of the *Hip Mama* community. Then, I extend theorists Lorna Stevens and Pauline McLaran's notion of women's print magazines as "dreamworlds" of femininity and consumption into cyber(cultural)space to explore the ways in which the hip mamas interact with dominant discourses of maternal consumption. I argue that *Hip Mama* functions as a text of sometimes opposing discourses linked together in cyberspaces. To further explore this, I turn to Bell's concept of the "hypertexual moment" (2). Bell states that a hypertextual moment is one that simultaneously holds different, often contradictory, narratives together at the same time (2). Thus, *Hip Mama*'s subversions and promotions of dominant discourses of maternity are only a click link away.

To examine the ways in which *Hip Mama* challenges conventional representations of maternity, I use a feminist lens of critical investigation. I also use discourse analysis and semiotic analysis to explore both epistemological and ontological suppositions that adhere to the texts. In these analyses, I investigate the ways in which maternal bodies are constructed within the *Hip Mama* website and explore which types of mothering are privileged or dismissed. As a researcher and forum participant, I have regularly been involved with *Hip Mama* since 1999. It is the site's feisty interrogation of normative representations of motherhood and constructions of outlaw maternity that have most caught my attention, and these features are the main focus of my discussion here.

HIP MAMA

The *Hip Mama* website, launched in 1997, is the cyberversion of the print zine of the same name. *Hip Mama's* mission statement proclaims it to be "a feminist, pro-choice, reader-written zine for progressive families" (Gore and Lavender). This alternative maternity community was founded by Ariel Gore, and the ezine is published by Bee Lavender. A self-described "welfare mother," Gore drew on her experiences as a teenage single mother in order to write and edit first the zine and then the book, *The Hip Mama's Survival Guide*. Throughout *Hip Mama's* incubation and early construction, Ariel Gore continued her studies and stated that motherhood increased rather than decreased her professional goals. Similarly, Lavender's biography—linked to *Hip Mama*—lists her considerable achievements gained despite the debilitating effects of illness and personal hardship. As a result of the popularity of their print and online publications, both Gore and Lavender are highly sought-after speakers about childraising concerns in both academic and mainstream forums.

In contrast to the earnest tone of mainstream mothering websites, *Hip Mama* writes a strongly political maternity and nonmainstream online community. The term "hip mama" is playfully described on the site as a maternal body that both acknowledges and moves beyond traditional representations of motherhood. In the "About Us" section, *Hip Mama* is described as "a magazine bursting with political commentary and ribald tales from the front lines of motherhood.... *Hip Mama* maintains the editorial vision that qualified it for the title 'conservative America's worst nightmare'"

(Lavender). Throughout the website, hip mamas are generally written as feminist, vegetarian, tattooed, pierced, and as political activists. This provides a contrast to the representations of well-groomed, product-hungry, irrevocably cheerful maternal bodies primarily appearing on commercialized maternity websites, such as *americanbaby.com* and *babycenter.com* (Goriss-Hunter). These websites construct maternal bodies as consumers, who are urged by "expert" intervention to buy maternity-oriented products and services to ensure the health and wellbeing of their family.

HIP MAMA OUTLAWS

In order to write, edit, and produce *Hip Mama*'s alternative maternity, Gore and Lavender draw on their past experiences as impoverished single mothers. Through their association with *Hip Mama*, however, both Gore and Lavender have morphed from "welfare moms" to celebrity personalities and poster girls for alternative motherhood grounded in a feminist sensibility. Together, Gore and Lavender are depicted in alternative and mainstream media as the hippest of the hip mamas (Brown; Tea). Despite their career success, fame, and affluence, I argue that their commitment to the writing of a political, creative, sexual, and raced maternity positions them as mother outlaws.

With the term "mother outlaw," Andrea O'Reilly (*Mother Outlaws*) takes up Adrienne Rich's division of motherhood into institution, as controlled by patriarchal narratives, and mother-centred discourse of maternal empowerment. Rich posits that if mothers reject patriarchal maternity and its central tenet of "powerless responsibility"—the (self)erasure of maternal voice, desire and body—they become "conspirators, outlaws from the institution of motherhood" (194-195). O'Reilly embraces Rich's arguments and contends that maternity is "not naturally, necessarily or inevitably oppressive" (*Mother Outlaws* 2); rather, it is the institution of motherhood that controls and limits maternal bodies. Both O'Reilly and Rich argue that when motherhood is removed from the restrictive status of patriarchal institution, it becomes a location of empowerment and social change for maternal bodies. For O'Reilly, empowered maternity "recognizes that both mothers and children benefit when the mother lives her life and practices mothering from a position of agency, authority, authenticity, and autonomy" (*Mother Outlaws* 12). Thus, empowered mothering transgresses norms of Western motherhood. It foregrounds maternal voices and desires while rejecting the white, middle-class ideal of intensive mothering with its strict child-centredness and negation of the mother-self.

Empowered mothering, as posited by Rich and O'Reilly, fuels an exuberant outlaw maternity that focuses on mother-centred narratives of agency and revels in breaking the masculinist laws of the father. Mother outlaws move beyond mainstream discourses of maternity to explore the possibilities of mothering narratives based on lived experience and context. The *Hip Mama* website celebrates a movement of mother outlaws into cyber(cultural) space and encourages a cyber-empowered maternity to emerge from its writings and community in two primary fashions. First, *Hip Mama* does not endorse the fantasy of the good mother that mainstream maternity magazines address. The ezine is written and produced by a number of politically aware feminists. Second, *Hip Mama* disrupts the traditional binaries of author-reader, producer-consumer, and appropriate-deviant maternal as contributors write personal narratives that employ modes of expression and deal with topics outside of conventional discourses of maternity.

On the website, hip mamas mobilize the DIY philosophy of zines in combination with a fiery alternative maternity to produce an ezine and linked sites that feature a lived politics of maternal bodies. This outlaw maternity is evident not only on *Hip Mama*'s main website but also throughout the ezine's three sister sites founded by Bee Lavender: *Yo Mama Says, Mamaphonic,* and *Girl-Mom.* The first of the sister sites, *Yo Mama Says,* embraces the mother outlaw in terms of politics. Contributors on this site write spiritedly against traditional tropes of apolitical maternity. Issues raised on this website include antiwar protests, campaigns to prevent the closure of women's health services, and "nurse-ins"—groups of breastfeeding mothers organized in response to negative reactions to breastfeeding in public. *Mamaphonic* encourages expressions of mother outlaws in terms of creativity. Participants on this site write back to conventional representations of maternity that limit maternal creativity to the domestic sphere. *Girl-Mom* evokes the mother outlaw that writes back to dominant narratives prescribing maternal age and the normative construction of teen parenting as inadequate and impoverished. *Yo Mama, Mamaphonic,* and *Girl-Mom* link to and from the blog-based *Hip Mama.* Together, these websites create an interactive community of maternal bodies that challenge traditional constructions.

The disruption of binaries on the *Hip Mama* website is bolstered by the emphasis on personal blogs and interaction, as opposed to the more impersonal feature articles that predominate in mainstream print and online magazines. There are regular postings that encourage hip mamas to write articles and share their opinions about topics that others have raised. The ezine is almost entirely constructed by and through interconnections and flows of sometimes contradictory ideas, beliefs, stories, and strategies as contributed by hip mamas. The focus on blog-based communication facilitates a sense of immediacy and connectivity that encourages the ability to interact, which strengthens community. It is in attempting the construction of a nonconforming online maternity community that *Hip Mama* and its participants demonstrate the ways in which a virtual group is able to go beyond dominant discourses of motherhood and community. They also show how durable these conventional narratives are in cybercommunities.

COMMUNITY

To interrogate the limits and boundaries of the *Hip Mama* community, I draw on the theories of Howard Rheingold and David Bell. Rheingold promotes the notion of virtual communities as "naturally" occurring in the new territory of cyberspace, as he argues that these groups fill the void left by the decline of the contemporary face-to-face community. Bell refutes Rheingold's conceptualization of virtual community as organic and natural. Bell argues that the forces of globalization, disembedding, in which social practices are increasingly shifting beyond local contexts, detraditionalization, and reflexivity encourage a contemporary form of online community that shifts beyond conventional ideas of communal groups and their expectations (95-97). Whereas Rheingold looks to a fantasy of an organically developing utopia to define the virtual community, Bell describes online communities as places of constant change, difference, and situational, often global, alliances. My investigation of virtual maternity communities suggests that the reality of online community formation and engagement is more complex than Rheingold allows in his analysis.

Hip Mama is a globally available online community that attracts postings from participants all over the world. Despite this immersion in flows of globalization, *Hip Mama* is also marked as a site that is grounded in a specific culture, as a significant proportion of the hip mamas live in or are citizens of the United States. This is obvious in the topics with which they engage and the language used. For instance, much discussion on the blogs centres around American politics and culture. American terms such as "kick-ass," "hard-rockin," and "diaper" are often used.

Although the disembeddedness of the *Hip Mama* community is modified by its distinctive North American orientation and the defining of group members according to various subject positions, the site's subversion of traditional tropes of maternity releases spirited narratives of outlaw mothering in cyber(cultural)space. This lawless contradiction of conventional maternity discourse is demonstrated in the topics of discussion threads that express a nonmainstream mothering. Maternity written as a diversity of experiences rather than traditional limitation is evidenced in the variety and type of topics covered in the feature articles, blogs, and postings of the *Hip Mama* site. A politically charged motherhood is suggested throughout the *Hip Mama* blogs, and they address a variety of issues, including biracial children, bankrupt alcoholic mothers, parenting without positive parental role models, domestic violence, the reporting of incidents involving breastfeeding mothers, and nonmainstream childrearing philosophies. Even in providing assistance grounded in lived experience, *Hip Mama* still addresses complex and charged topics, such as retaining custody, extracting child support from reluctant sources, and instituting restraining orders on abusive ex-partners. The subversive mothering subjects discussed on the *Hip Mama* site stand in sharp contrast to the popular topics of interest in the commercial and more mainstream maternity websites, such as *americanbaby.com* and *babycenter.com*

(Brown; Goriss-Hunter). In the latter websites, conventional maternity narratives are reflected in the popularity of topics of articles, blogs, and forums that focus on maternal bodies being responsible for maintaining "appropriate" weight, ensuring family health and safety, and keeping up to date with fashion (Goriss-Hunter). This focus on conventional maternity narratives is even reflected in the titles of articles and forums—such as "How to Lose Belly Fat After Having a Baby," "Beauty Tips for Time Poor Mums," "Bargain Hunters," and "Cooking for Your Family".

The hip mamas' outlaw status in the rejection of conventional maternity discourse is also apparent in the pointed focus on diverse maternal sexuality. Posts discuss hip mamas' partnered and nonpartnered, same-sex, and heterosexual relationships. In her blog, Ariel Gore publicly documents her own same-sex relationship. Writers are often supportive of same-sex relationships, and heteronormativity is frequently critiqued. The hip mamas' movement beyond the heteronormative assumptions that are explicit on mainstream mothering websites and magazines is important in two areas. First, it speaks to the silence throughout conventional motherhood websites concerning maternal sexuality in general. Second, this shift also creates space for the expression of a range of sexualities rather than the narratives of heterosexuality, which are strongly intertwined with imperatives to consume on the more commercialized maternity websites.

To further explore the intermeshing of consumption, dominant discourse, and critique throughout *Hip Mama,* I extend theorists Lorna Stevens and Pauline McLaran's notion of women's print magazines as "dreamworlds" of femininity and consumption into cyber(cultural)space. Stevens and Maclaran posit that the conflation of femininity, shopping, and consumption encouraged by women's magazines and department stores facilitates the creation of a "shopping imaginary," in which readers consume in ways that rely on imagination, aspiration, and fantasy (283-284). According to the authors, the harnessing of consumer desire by the production of a variety of goods, services, and information enables the reader to play with meanings and identities. Thus, consumption operates on two levels within women's print and online magazines: the literal consuming of the text and the goods and services promoted in it as well as the anticipation and promotion of desire (Stevens and McLaran 283-284).

Although the dreamworlds of commercialized mothering websites focus on the desiring and consumption of specific goods and services as well as traditional narratives of motherhood, the hip mamas' shopping imaginary supports robust and humorous challenges to dominant maternal discourses. In their dreamworld, the hip mamas play with the commodity-driven maternity of mainstream mothering websites by pointing out the absurdity of their heteronormative and commercial motherhood. One hip mama posted a link on Ariel Gore's site to her own one, in which she sells a variety of clothes for adults, children, and babies—all emblazoned with the slogan "My other mother is also a lesbian." This construction of an out-law maternity allows for a detraditionalization of the conventional maternal bodies constructed in mainstream maternity sites, as even the shopping dreamworld or economy of the hip mamas expresses moments of cultural critique and humour.

Despite the rejection of narratives of commercialized motherhood, *Hip Mama*'s advertisements and calls for subscriptions demonstrate that even noncommercial maternity ezines do not operate outside the financial considerations that ensure the viability of an Internet publication. The tensions between the reality of financing a website and *Hip Mama*'s anti-commercial stance fuel a shopping dreamworld of paradox. In contrast to the hypercommercialism of mainstream maternity websites, *Hip Mama* writes directly about the need for financial support to allow the site to continue. *Hip Mama* acknowledges the inevitable imbrication of commerce and e-text on the Internet and directly appeals to the participant to "Get rid of the ads! Subscribe to the site!"

The hip mamas enjoy a shopping dreamworld that is much less glossy than those on mainstream mothering websites but is also dependent on commercial consumption. Advertisements are relegated to one column on the left side of the *Hip Mama* site as well as the *Hip Mama Shop*, which is hypertexted from the home page. These advertisements regularly change as sponsorship deals are made, renewed, or ended. In May 2009, *Hip Mama* advertised books from a self-publishing company, from various educational institutions, and from Earth-Justice, a nonprofit public interest law firm. The *Hip Mama* shop sells merchandise directly related to the site: books written by the hip mamas and t-shirts advertising these texts. This mix of commodity-driven maternity magazine—somewhat similar to the commercialism of mainstream motherhood sites—and alternative ezine critiquing the forces of commerciality sits uneasily together in a shopping dreamworld that attempts to combine opposing discourses of commercial and alternative maternity.

Although the hip mamas' refusal of the commercial aspects of mainstream maternity websites is not complete, the strong desire to overturn traditional notions of maternal bodies and to rework concepts of community in the process continues to surface in discussions. The hip mamas' position outside normative motherhood, and their desire to "belong" in a group where difference is embraced, is expressed in the *Hip Mama* website by imagining a contemporary "urban tribe" of hip mamas or "alterna-moms" who choose to be members of a virtual nonconformist maternity community.

WILL THE REAL HIP MAMA PLEASE WRITE BACK!

Unlike the posts on commercialized maternity websites, where sustained reflexive discussion concerning maternal subject positions is limited (Goriss-Hunter), the hip mamas debate and attempt to define the meanings they attach to the term "hip mama." For instance, in a discussion thread in January 2004 concerning the definition of the maternal subject of *Hip Mama*, there are three positions that the hip mamas define themselves against: the soccer mom, the yuppie mama, and the Sunday school mama, who is steeped in conservative morality and moralizing behaviour. In one *Hip Mama* blog "hipness" is constructed as all that is not conventional and against the notion of the "soccer mom":

> I do feel more drawn to the alterna-moms out there regardless. And it is exciting to me to realize that I am still the same somewhat cool and interesting woman who had lots of interests and pursuits before Joey (child) came along. Sometimes I need to remind myself of that. Like I am not

going to suddenly just morph into some conservative soccer mom. (sidenote: if J does wind up playing soccer, however, I will be there every Sat. morning to cheer for him!)

This post as well as other *Hip Mama* blogs and articles echo Adrienne Rich's conceptualization of motherhood as a construction of separate yet simultaneously occurring aspects, which incorporate a restrictive institution and an empowering strand of possibilities. In this particular example, the blogger refuses to assume the mantle of over-availability and negation of desire implicit in the subject position of the "soccer mom." However, the hip mama acknowledges her own potential desire to act as a "soccer mom" if her son began to play soccer in order to support him and participate in his life. The hip mama's comment abounds with complexity and demonstrates the impossibility of ever being completely unaffected by narratives of conventional mothering. Within this acknowledgement of the ever-present institution of motherhood, however, the hip mama rejects conventional maternity (soccer mom) to the extent she is able to, and embraces the potentially empowering strand of the maternal: a positive connection with the children. Thus, the hip mama in this example conceptualizes contemporary motherhood in terms of empowering potential that is willingly assumed by maternal bodies, whereas the convention-institution strand is present but abandoned where possible.

In the post previously cited, the author further explores the alternative status of the hip mamas. She writes:

> maybe I'm not a "hipmama." I mean I think I am hip. (I have a tattoo! I am a liberal feminist almost-vegetarian! I am a Witch!) But. I don't feel as hip as some of these hard-rockin', multiple piercings, goth-type mamas out there. I have a bit of a standard job, married my wonderful h.s [high school] sweetheart, and dress mostly pretty run of the mill comfy, though sometimes a bit more funky and fun. I guess there are varying degrees.

Of the ten responses to this blog, nine writers supported the blogger's divided position concerning the constitution of hip mamadom, which further fractures traditional tropes of maternity along lines that both use and reject the conventional maternal. A number of participants reassured the author of the post that she was, in fact, "hip." For instance, in that same 2004 discussion, another hip mama writes that

> Being "hip" to me has nothing to do with what I call plea-sure preferences—whether you dress Goth or Goodwill, listen to the Clash or classical, or whether you have a nose ring or a pearl ring. But being "hip" means tolerating all of these differences and understanding that people make their own, private choices that they feel best suits them and realizing that those choices may not always mesh with your own sensibilities.

These comments attempt to undo the roping of the term "hip" to a very particular subjectivity—tattoos, piercings, artistic work, and a politics for the nonprivileged—and then link the word to a broadly encompassing liberal framework. The postings broaden the notion of hip to go beyond the popular definition of fashion and trendiness.

The site's blogs, however, also inscribe a particular subjectivity that stands for a "hip mama," which reveals the limits of this community. Although the hip mamas challenge conventions in general, and traditional maternity specifically, they are also partially entangled in mainstream narratives of the maternal. A significant number of hip mamas who post personal blogs express support for dominant discourses, including the following: child-centred practices or intensive mothering, the regulation of female body size, and children inheriting the father's last name.

Hip mamas are also not immune to the lure of aspirational desires to fulfil idealized notions of bourgeois achievement or to transcend the limitations of class, culture, and financial cir-cumstance. Middle-class aspirational goals—such as obtaining a tertiary education, working in a professional career, and financial security—are foregrounded in the personal blogs. The "rags to riches" stories of Lavender and Gore also fulfil aspirational fan-tasies of the American Dream. It is in the narratives of "dream fulfilment," as well as the broadening of notions of "hip" to include discourses of bourgeois desires and attainment, that *Hip Mama* continues a subtle movement towards narratives of conventional motherhood and mainstream maternity e-texts. The gradual shift demonstrates how the traditional is imported into predominantly alternative online communities, in which, as Bell argues, numerous sometimes contradictory narratives exist hypertextually. This hypertexting of dominant discourse and unconventional narratives also illustrates the inevitable diversity of online communities and motherhood itself.

HIP MAMA TOWN

In a series of postings from June 2005 some hip mamas express a desire for *Hip Mama* participants to move to a small town and populate it with members of this online community. On 23 June 2005, a hip mama began the thread by writing: "Let's all move to a little dying town somewhere and make it a hipmama town. Why not? Our kids could all run around together, we could make a kickass school Community garden? Regular community meals?" This post inspired one of the largest threads in the *Hip Mama* blogs with fifty-four responses. Reinvigorating a "dying town somewhere" with a "hip mama" presence echoes notions at the cornerstone of Rheingold's theories—contemporary face-to-face communities are "dying" and need to be revived, and cybercommunities perform this task.

The hip mama longings to transform online community into groups that meet in person reinvest the notion of community with utopian Rheingoldian narratives. Community—online and in person—is then fetishized and essentialized as positive for everyone. This nostalgic desire speaks of the difficulty of living a maternity that challenges norms in a culture saturated by dominant discourses of motherhood.

In the discussion thread concerning setting up a hip mama town, a number of posts detail concerns about the successful translation of the virtual community to a face-to-face environment in which inhabitants would be unable to leave the group in absolute terms by logging out of online space. In a 2005 blog, a hip mama writes that "I just think that our many differences, while tolerable in a virtual community would not be tolerated in a real life community." Issues of differing philosophies and tensions along lines of childrearing practices as well as class and race were foregrounded in a number of posts.

The tensions and conflicts evident in the blogs concerning community demonstrate that maternity is not a universal state. It is dependent on context, as maternal bodies are the locus for intersections of sometimes competing discourses of gender, sexuality, class, and race. Similarly, virtual communities, especially those concerned with maternal bodies, are not utopias of maternity created from the popularised and traditional notion of the "common bonds of motherhood." As with communities that meet in person, virtual communities are, as Bell argues, fraught with conflict, differences, and competing desires.

CONCLUSIONS

Standing outside much of the mainstream face-to-face and online maternal community life, hip mamas reflexively consider and critique discourses of maternity. Their irreverent take on maternity extends Andrea O'Reilly's notion of the mother outlaw into cyber(cultural)space. They attempt to fulfil their desire for nonmainstream communities by the attempted detraditionalization of online gatherings to promote subversive versions of conventional motherhood. *Hip Mama*'s reworking of the content and format of the zine into a vibrant ezine promotes discourses of maternal politics, sexuality, and creativity. These narratives assist in the construction of an alternative *Hip Mama* body and online maternity community. The *Hip Mama* body and community, however, are fractured along many lines, including lifestyle, personal style, desire for universality, and class. The moments of dissent written in the *Hip Mama* posts aptly demonstrate the fragmentedness of online maternity communities as opposed to myths of universal narratives of motherhood and community. Although the hip mamas open up space for narratives of unorthodox maternity and attempt to form a new kind of community, threads of longing or immersion in conventional motherhood still emerge. Even though these strands of traditional motherhood flow through the site, *Hip Mama*'s vibrant and witty challenge to mainstream maternity ensures that the website is still a vital cyber-threat to the dusty narratives of traditional motherhood. The cyber-mother-outlaws of *Hip Mama* continue to rework conventional images of maternal bodies while simultaneously being haunted by the spectre of the "good mother." In so doing, the hip mamas present a cybermaternity that is diverse, situated, and is lived hypertextually.

WORKS CITED

Bargain Hunters. *BabyCenter*. http://community.babycenter.com/groups/a25/bargain_hunters. Accessed 24 Jan. 2015.

Bell, David. *An Introduction to Cybercultures*. Routledge, 2001.

Brown, Michael. "An Interview with Ariel Gore & Bee Lavender of *Hip Mama*." *Serials Review*, vol. 28, no. 2, 2002, pp. 159-162.

Cooking for your family. *BabyCenter*. http://community.babycenter.com/groups/a535/cooking_for_your_family. Accessed 24 Jan, 2015.

Gore, Ariel, and Bee Lavender. *Hip Mama*, 2016, hipmama.com. Accessed 27 Aug. 2016.

Gore, Ariel. *The Hip Mama Survival Guide: Advice from the Trenches on Pregnancy, Childbirth, Cool Names, Clueless Doctors, Potty Training and Toddler Avengers*. Hyperion Books, 1987.

Goriss-Hunter, Anitra. "You Can Visit Hotel Mommy: Maternal Bodies as Browsing/Consuming Biotourists." *Journal of Gender Studies*, vol. 25, no. 1, 2016, pp. 85-98.

"How to Lose Belly Fat after Having a Baby." *Belly Belly*, Bellybelly, 17 Apr. 2015, bellybelly.com. Accessed 26 Apr. 2016.

Humphry, J. "Beauty Tips for Time Poor Mums." *Mum's Lounge*. Mum's Lounge, 6 July, 2015, www.mumslounge.com.au/lifestyle/mums-thumbs-up/beauty-tips-for-time-poor-mums-plus-join-us-in-momentsforme-to-win-an-indulgent-spa-treatment/. Accessed 5 Sept. 2015.

Lavender, Bee. "About Us." *Hip Mama*, Hip Mama, 8 Jan 2005, hipmama.com. Accessed 14 Mar. 2008.

O'Reilly, Andrea. *Feminist Mothering*. SUNY Press, 2008. Print.

O'Reilly, Andrea. *From Motherhood to Mothering: The Legacy of Adrienne Rich's* Of Woman Born. SUNY Press, 2004.

O'Reilly, Andrea. *Mother Outlaws: Theories and Practices of Empowered Mothering*. Women's Press, 2004.

Rheingold, Howard. *Virtual Community: Homesteading on the Electronic Frontier*. Addison Wesley, 1993.

Rich, Adrienne. *Of Woman Born: Motherhood as Experience and Institution*. Virago, 1977.

Stevens, Lorna., and Pauline Maclaran. "Exploring the 'shopping imaginary': The Dreamworld of Women's Magazines." *Journal of Consumer Behaviour*, vol. 4, no. 4, 2005, pp. 282-292.

Tea, Michelle. "The Hippest Mama: MUTHA Interviews Ariel Gore." *MUTHA Magazine*, 18 Sept. 2013, *Muthamagazine.com*. Accessed 15 Apr. 2016.

10.
Virtual Outlaws

Feminist Motherhood on the Internet

JOCELYN CRAIG

THERE ARE MANY GROUPS AND SPACES for mothers online where women gather to find community and share advice and information on mothering. Most of these spaces—from social networking sites for mothers to online parenting magazines and mommy blogs—tend to replicate and reinforce patriarchal ideals of motherhood, but some feminist mothers have begun to create online spaces specifically intended to resist and challenge these ideals. In this chapter, I will explore the potential of various online mothering spaces in relation to the goals of what Andrea O'Reilly has termed "outlaw motherhood," defined as "an oppositional stance that seeks to counter and correct the many ways in which patriarchal motherhood causes mothering to be limiting or oppressive to women" (20). In particular, I will examine explicitly feminist mothering groups and their capacity to recreate and expand the project of feminist consciousness-raising towards the possibility of empowered and emancipated feminist motherhood for the twenty-first century.

NEW POSSIBILITIES FOR RESISTANCE

In her groundbreaking book *Of Woman Born*, first published in 1976, Adrienne Rich describes "two meanings of motherhood, one superimposed on the other: the *potential relationship* of any woman to her powers of reproduction and to children; and the *institution*, which aims at ensuring that that potential—and all women—shall remain under male control" (13). The patriarchal institution of motherhood encompasses the organization of society around the nuclear family unit (an arrangement that leaves women vulnerable to isolation and male violence); social welfare policy that engenders women's economic dependence on individual men; and the myriad of cultural expectations governing what mothers must be and do in order to be considered "good enough." In her book *The Cultural Contradictions of Motherhood*, Sharon Hays describes these expectations using the term "intensive mothering," an ideology that says that good mothering must be "child-centered, expert-guided, emotionally absorbing, labor-intensive, and financially expensive" (8).

The institution of motherhood circumscribes women's lives and choices as mothers. An important aspect of patriarchal motherhood is that it is isolating (Drentea and Moren-Cross 921). Whether mothers participate in the paid workforce or not, they are expected to centre their lives around home and family. Increasing rates of wealth inequality and of single motherhood can make it especially difficult for women to connect with one another and discuss these issues; the Internet, however, has opened new possibilities for community and feminist engagement.

The advent of social media has allowed for greater access to feminist ideas and information (Crane 14). Using the Internet, mothers are free to connect with one another independent of their children, with online interactions less fragmented by the distraction of children than those occurring in person (Friedman 355-356). Tracey Kennedy argues that the Internet provides a new means for women to come together in the spirit of feminist consciousness-raising, which fosters intimacy and builds community among women who can then act collectively towards creating social change.

Despite these positive developments, the possibilities for feminist mothering created by the Internet are tempered by issues of access relating to literacy, geographic location, and socioeconomic status. Participation may be further limited by marginalization stemming from the white, married, heterosexual, middle-class norms that tend to dominate most online mothering spaces (Chen 515; Friedman 357). Even so, for mothers who have access, the Internet has opened critical opportunities for the possibility of collective resistance to the patriarchal institution of motherhood.

MY SEARCH FOR FEMINIST MOTHERING SPACES

When I became pregnant with my first child in 2007, few of my friends had children. Hoping to find information and support, I began to look online for spaces where I could ask questions and interact with other moms. Over the course of my pregnancy, my partner, the father of my child, became increasingly controlling and, eventually, violent. By the time I left him for good, when my daughter was just eleven days old, I was desperately in need of another kind of support. I began to turn to feminist spaces online in a quest to better understand what had happened to me, and why it was happening to so many women in my own country and across the globe. I found many helpful spaces, mostly blogs and groups, where women came together to discuss such issues as patriarchy, rape culture, and sexism in the media; yet I found that both domestic violence and motherhood were (perhaps surprisingly, given the number of women affected by these issues[1]) rarely prominent topics of discussion in these spaces.

The online spaces for mothers that I found—including social media sites, groups, and blogs—seemed to recapitulate and reinforce the patriarchal ideologies that I was struggling against, whereas the explicitly feminist spaces tended to largely ignore topics pertinent to mothers and mothering. It finally occurred to me to start searching for feminist spaces that were specifically for moms. At first, I found it difficult to find spaces that were active. Some had not had any new posts for months. But eventually, I discovered a small handful of groups and spaces that seemed to offer the possibility of support, resistance, and a way forwards for would-be outlaw mothers like me. In the next section, I discuss some of the types of online mothering spaces that I encountered and explain why feminist mothering groups, in which members explicitly locate and examine their experiences within the context of patriarchal motherhood, are a valuable tool in the project of outlaw motherhood.

REDEFINING MOTHERHOOD?

Social Networking Sites for Mothers
In the past decade, numerous social networking websites and

message boards geared towards mothers have appeared online. Researchers studying these sites have found that although they can be an important source of social and emotional support, especially for new mothers, they tend to reify gendered inequality and reinforce the nuclear family structure through the uncritical reproduction of patriarchal norms of motherhood (Drentea and Moren-Cross 940; Madge and O'Connor 212). May Friedman suggests that when patriarchal motherhood is replicated in online spaces, it tends to happen in two ways: "first, with the majority of the performance of motherhood on the Internet documenting and reproducing the conditions of patriarchal motherhood, and second, with the predominance of elitist voices on motherhood potentially erasing empowered or otherwise non-normative experiences from the lexicon of maternal behavior" (355). My own explorations of mothering sites—such as the popular social networking site *CafeMom*, launched in 2006—have tended to confirm these observations.

Mommy Blogging

At the BlogHer conference in San Jose, California, in 2005, Alice Bradley, a popular so-called mommy blogger, declared, "Mommy blogging is a radical act!" (qtd. in Lopez 730). Lori Lopez contends that mommy blogging is a form of community building that subverts women's usual reliance on male experts for information and advice on raising children (743). She further argues that it challenges and expands traditional notions of motherhood and that by "showing the ugly side of motherhood, [it] has the potential to be liberating and beneficial for all women" (744). Echoing the concerns of many mommy bloggers, Gina Chen asserts that the empowerment that women may derive from blogging about their experiences as mothers may be undermined by the very term "mommy blogger," with its diminutive and limiting implications, although she nonetheless agrees with Bradley that "the experience of writing about one's family, children, and life can be a radically empowering act" (Chen 511).

In contrast to these optimistic visions, Kara Van Cleaf explores mommy blogging in the context of neoliberalism and with attention to the aims of feminist consciousness-raising groups in the 1970s (247). She contrasts the personal writings on motherhood by Rich in *Of Woman Born* with that of present-day mommy bloggers and finds that "the feminist project of situating women's experiences within a larger social context as a way to effect change, as so adroitly done by Rich, has disappeared" (248). Van Cleaf argues that despite Alice Bradley's bold declaration, mommy bloggers generally do not incorporate a critique of patriarchal norms of motherhood into their writing; instead, they treat their challenges as personal and individual, but that fails to connect the personal with the political (248-250). In the neoliberal context, as Van Cleaf asserts, the personal is no longer political but has instead become a commodity wherein women's intimate experiences are transformed into "likes," "shares," and advertising revenue, which produces economic value for decidedly unfeminist interests (255). Like social media sites for mothers, mommy blogs offer important opportunities for connection and community, yet on the whole, this research suggests that mommy blogs may reinforce patriarchal and neoliberal values, even as they purport to challenge them.

Feminist Mothering Groups

In the late 1960s and early 1970s, many women organized and participated in what they called consciousness-raising groups. The purpose of these groups was for women to come together and share their personal experiences in order to place those experiences within the larger context of women's shared oppression as women. As Carol Hanisch states in her 1969 essay "The Personal is Political": "One of the first things we discover in these groups is that personal problems are political problems. There are no personal solutions at this time. There is only collective action for a collective solution." In contrast to mainstream mothering boards and mommy blogs, some feminist mothers have begun to create spaces where the intent is to go beyond "unmasking motherhood" (Maushart 2) or providing social and emotional support and community (although these are also important aspects of the groups) in order to explicitly and intentionally situate mothers' experiences within the context of patriarchal motherhood. In other words, the aim is to locate the problems of motherhood under patriarchy as collective problems requiring a collective solution.

173

I have explored several such groups and spaces as I have discovered them, but my favourite is a group called *Feminist Mothers*.[2] The by-invitation-only group was founded in 2013 by Lauren, an Australian feminist single mother of two. She became frustrated with the lack of support for mothers in other feminist spaces, and she wanted to create a space that centred issues of motherhood under patriarchy. The act of mothers writing and talking about their lives and concerns has often been criticized for lacking seriousness or importance. At the same BlogHer conference where Bradley called mommy blogging "a radical act," another woman suggested that if women "stopped blogging about themselves they could change the world" (qtd. in Lopez 732). Similarly, Lauren and others had found that their perspectives as mothers were often trivialized or even derided within other feminist groups and spaces; it was frustration with this situation that led Lauren to found *Feminist Mothers*. The enthusiastic response she received confirmed her feeling that such a space was sorely needed.

Members of Feminist Mothers hail from a number of different countries, including Canada, Australia, the UK, the U.S., and New Zealand. Participants use a feminist lens to discuss and debate a variety of topics, including domestic and sexual violence, parenting styles, birthing practices, media and entertainment, current events, and feminist theory. Although members differ in terms of race, class, age, sexuality, nationality, and other axes of identity, many have had similar experiences with abuse, male violence, and legal systems that seem designed to protect male control over women and children at the expense of their safety and wellbeing. These experiences are embedded within the patriarchal institution of motherhood; an analysis of how mothers are constrained and harmed by this institution is often a central theme of discussion.

Many women in *Feminist Mothers* feel that the experience of mothering has been an important catalyst in developing their feminist consciousness. Some members came to feminism after their experiences of abuse. Lauren, speaking of her experiences with the family court system, criminal justice system, and welfare system after escaping from a violent husband, says, "It is not until faced with these systems that you really understand the essence of patriarchy."[3] For others, the experience of mothering imparted a sense of urgency in addressing issues of injustice for women. Grace, another member, says, "[Becoming a mother] made me realize I don't have time to dilly dally—my daughter in particular needs the world to change now. Being a mother radicalized me."

When I ask members about their participation in *Feminist Mothers* via an online interview-conversation, many emphasize the importance of the group in their lives as a place to seek and offer support, as a source of validation for their frustrations and struggles, and as a way to stay connected with other women when they feel isolated as mothers. Serena describes the feelings of many members when she says, "This group is the one constant place of sanity I have online and one of the only ones in my life. You women are wise and angry and true. I feel [at] home here. I wish I could be with you all in a real living room somewhere, but in the absence of that, I'll come to this virtual living room often for commiseration, succor, and love."

Group members also express a sense that participation in the group affects their mothering in positive ways. As Nicole puts it, "[This group] makes me stronger in my convictions to lead my children by feminist mothering—to nurture and speak fundamental truths beyond the patriarchy." And Karen says, "The conversations [here] have enabled me to reflect on and challenge my own thinking on many subjects. [They have] encouraged me to think through my own perspective and reasoning and to examine how the patriarchy can invade my own thought processes."

In many ways, unlike so many other mothering spaces online, *Feminist Mothers* and similar groups serve as spaces for virtual consciousness-raising, which help members to think critically about their lives and experiences and unearth the many ways in which the personal is political. Such critical thinking enables participants to think beyond what exists now in order to imagine what could be. Through the sharing of news articles, popular memes and quotes, personal stories, and other items, members examine the institution of motherhood and how it operates; they often uncover and suggest possible paths towards outlaw motherhood.

Informed by their interaction and participation in the group, members describe their ideas and visions of a practice of mothering that is free from patriarchal control. Nicole says, "A matriarchal society would be creative and thriving, rather than the current patriarchal system where it is about power, control, and ownership of others." Jennifer says, "Women would not struggle alone to try to keep their kids safe from an abuser, but would have community support where they would have the actual ability to say 'No.'" Lauren suggests, "Women would communally support other women, and raising children would be part of daily accepted life and not designated to individual mothers."

Several women describe the importance of abolishing legal paternity in favour of a more community-based concept of kinship. Such a structure would offer women greater support and protection from violence and economic insecurity, and men would freely provide guidance and care out of a desire to participate in children's lives rather than from a will to exercise power over women and children. Christine considers ideas derived from matrilineal and matrilocal cultures:

> The concept of "private property" was limited to personal and household possessions, and womyn, particularly womyn with children, were the holders of the home itself. So, if a man in a relationship with a mother found his personal possessions outside the home, he knew himself to be divorced and he could go live [in the] same village with his maternal relations or other solo men. No stigma of divorce for anyone, no putting children through that mess, no harm done to children's—or anyone's—primary relational bonds.

Serena offers, "I think imagining a new architecture could literally restructure the way we live. Small dwellings circled around a large common living area, for instance." Aside from creatively reimagining the relational and physical structures that define families, members question the way that we—as adults and parents— relate to children as people. Grace says, "We need to listen more to children themselves and respect them as beings. I never assume I know more than my children—I try to guide them when there are safety concerns but mostly I think my job is to teach them to listen to their inner wisdom and instincts and to not perpetuate the dysfunctions I was raised with.

Through conversations such as these, the members of *Feminist Mothers* can not only analyze their shared (and differing) experiences of motherhood under patriarchy but also collectively re-envision the possibilities that mothering holds. Together, members imagine how feminist mothers may work together to move towards a practice of outlaw motherhood, both within our own lives and as a community, as mothers search together for collective solutions to the collective problem of patriarchal motherhood.

CONCLUSIONS

Although most spaces for mothers online tend to replicate patriarchal ideals of motherhood, groups such as *Feminist Mothers* have explicitly challenged and resisted these ideals in the spirit of feminist consciousness-raising. By incorporating a feminist analysis of motherhood and patriarchy into the fabric of group discussions and connecting the personal with the political, these groups can go beyond the social and emotional support invited by the unmasking of mothers' everyday experiences and feelings to open additional possibilities for meaningful change. Groups like *Feminist Mothers* allow mothers to connect in ways that would not have been possible before the Internet, to share the company of other "outlaws from the institution of motherhood" (Rich 195) in circumstances where it would otherwise be difficult or impossible to gather in groups because of time limitations, lack of childcare, physical distance, and other factors. Access to technology is still limited by economic status and geographic location, but for feminist mothers who are able to use the Internet at home, these spaces are a lifeline—a source of validation and support, and a vital resource for moving towards a practice of mothering that is woman and child centred and free from patriarchal control.

In the years since I first embarked on the journey of motherhood as a single mother and survivor of domestic violence, I have repartnered and now have two daughters. Online spaces continue to be an important source of connection with other feminist moms.

For me, Feminist Mothers has been a vital source of friendship and community. It has deepened my understanding of both the differences and commonalities that mothers share in a number of different circumstances and locations. It is a place of comfort for when I feel overwhelmed or despairing, but most importantly, it is a place of hope for the possibilities of a world transformed by feminist practice.

NOTES

[1]As of 2010, 81 percent of U.S. women aged forty to forty-four had become mothers ("Facts for Features"). According to the Center for Disease Control and Prevention's National Intimate Partner and Sexual Violence Survey, one in three U.S. women will experience physical violence by an intimate partner at some point in her life (Black et al. 38).

[2]The name of the group has been changed to protect the privacy of its members, and all members have been given pseudonyms.

[3]All quotes from members of Feminist Mothers in this chapter are taken from a group conversation that occurred in September 2015.

WORKS CITED

Black, Michele C et al. *The National Intimate Partner and Sexual Violence Survey: 2010 Summary Report. Centers for Disease Control and Prevention*, U.S. Department of Health and Human Services, Nov. 2011, www.cdc.gov/violenceprevention/nisvs/. Accessed 10 Apr. 2016.

Chen, G. M. "Don't Call Me That: A Techno-Feminist Critique of the Term Mommy Blogger." *Mass Communication and Society*, vol. 16, no. 4, 2013, pp. 510-532.

Crane, Connie Jeske. "Social Media as a Feminist Tool." *Herizons*, vol. 26, no. 2, 2012, pp. 14-16.

Drentea, Patricia, and Jennifer L. Moren-Cross. "Social Capital and Social Support on the Web: The Case of an Internet Mother Site." *Sociology of Health & Illness*, vol. 27, no. 7 2005, pp. 920-943.

"Facts for Features: Mother's Day: May 13, 2012." *The United*

States Census Bureau, U.S. Census Bureau, 19 Mar. 2012, www.census.gov/newsroom/releases/archives/facts_for_features_special_editions/cb12-ff08.html. Accessed 11 Apr. 2016.

Friedman, May. "It Takes a (Virtual) Village: Mothering on the Internet." *Twenty-First Century Motherhood: Experience, Identity, Policy, Agency*, edited by Andrea O'Reilly, Columbia University Press, 2010, pp. 352-365.

Hanisch, Carol. "The Personal is Political." *Carol Hanisch*, Carol Hanisch, 2008, carolhanisch.org. Accessed 27 Nov. 2015.

Hays, Sharon. *The Cultural Contradictions of Motherhood*. Yale University Press, 1996.

Kennedy, Tracy L. M. "The Personal is Political: Feminist Blogging and Virtual Consciousness-Raising." *Scholar and Feminist Online*, vol., no. 5, 2007, http://sfonline.barnard.edu/blogs/kennedy_01.htm. Accessed 27 Nov. 2015.

Lopez, Lori. "The Radical Act of 'Mommy Blogging': Redefining Motherhood through the Blogosphere." *New Media & Society*, vol. 11, no. 5, 2009, pp. 729-747.

Madge, Clare, and Henrietta O'Connor. "Parenting Gone Wired: Empowerment of New Mothers on the Internet?" *Social & Cultural Geography*, vol. 7, no. 2, 2006, pp. 199-220.

Maushart, Susan. *The Mask Of Motherhood: How Becoming a Mother Changes Everything and Why We Pretend It Doesn't*. Norton, 1999.

O'Reilly, Andrea. "Outlaw Motherhood: A Theory and Politic of Maternal Empowerment for the Twenty-First Century." *Hecate*, vol. 36, no. 1-2, 2010, pp. 17-29.

Rich, Adrienne. *Of Woman Born: Motherhood as Experience and Institution*. 2nd ed., Norton, 1986.

Van Cleaf, Kara. "*Of Woman Born* to Mommy Blogged: The Journey from the Personal as Political to the Personal as Commodity." *Women's Studies Quarterly*, vol. 43, no. 3-4, 2015, pp. 247-264.

11.
Feminist Parenting Online

Community, Contestation, and Change

MEIKA LOE, TESS CUMPSTONE, AND SUSAN B. MILLER

HOW DO PARENTS RESIST THE GENDERING of their children and build community around feminist parenting? Emily Kane's interview-based research on navigating the "gender trap" finds that many parents make efforts to loosen gendered constraints for their children and to engage in a variety of behaviours that reproduce traditionally gendered childhoods. Her research suggests that community support for non-normative gendering may not exist for most parents. But what if it did? Our research examines the world of feminist parenting bloggers who provide a community of support and online activism for those parents who are "resisters" and "innovators," and for those who recognize and disrupt gender, as defined by Kane.

This research treats feminist parenting bloggers as informal participant observers in the world of childrearing. In their blog posts, these parents reflect on their attempts to disrupt gender on an everyday level. Not only are they a key source of information and community for parents, but their weblogs (blogs) are also an often-overlooked site for research on feminist parenting. Based on our research using ethnographic methods and content analysis over the course of two years, we argue that feminist parenting blogs are important fields for envisioning and practising everyday equality, dismantling rigid gender roles, participating in online community activism, and parenting with an intersectional focus. Feminist parenting bloggers are social media activists employing consciousness-raising and community organizing tactics. The online communities created by these bloggers have the potential to create real political and social change. In this chapter, after providing historical background on feminist parenting blogs and a discussion of methods, we analyze how these bloggers 1) do feminism in families; 2) counter isolation and build community online; 3) negotiate internal and external obstacles to online community; and 4) sustain their activism offline.

FEMINIST PARENTING BLOGS

Most parenting blogs offer heteronormative, nuclear-family-centred, and traditionally gendered perspectives (Friedman and Calixte 29; see also Orton-Johnson in this volume). However, blogs that do not support the traditional power structure are often written by parents who identify as feminists. These feminist parenting blogs cover and intersect with a wide range of topics but most address gender inequality in society and point out those institutions that uphold structures of domination. The blogs in our sample are concerned with issues relating to social inequality and focus on raising children with social justice values.

Feminist blogging is a relatively recent growth field; of the thirty-six total blogs that we identified, twenty-one were started in the period between 2009 and 2012. According to research published in the *Guardian*, during this period, women built highly influential networks online by creating communities and doing product reviews (Pippert). Although bloggers have been critiqued as being "me-centred," especially "mommy bloggers," feminist parenting bloggers generally approach parenting as activism (Lopez 730). A typical feminist parenting blog makes gender a focus and usually has a primary author who writes about daily experiences raising a child. We found that most feminist parenting blogs also contain these specific elements: 1) critique of gender socialization; 2) a social equality premise in parenting that may involve other aspects of identity; 3) gender neutral or gender equal parenting advice; 4) advice for others on raising nonsexist children, including product and book reviews; and 5) a blog post that defines feminism or the blogger's values and identifies how the blogger will apply this lens to parenting.

Combining the identities of feminist and mother-parent is a radical act, and one that is rarely acknowledged by other nonparent feminist bloggers. This is also lost among the mainstream mommy bloggers, who may lack critical perspective or agree with the dominant ideology when it comes to mothering. In a conversation with *Ms. Magazine*, several feminist parenting bloggers discussed "a heated debate online about how feminism welcomes or ignores mothering issues." This was spurred on by two articles published in 2009 in *The Nation* and *The Guardian* discussing the intersection of mothering and feminism (Nathman). These national and global discussions catalyzed feminist parenting bloggers. In the years after these publications, the number of feminist parenting bloggers increased dramatically, and many weighed in, via our questionnaires, on how being a feminist parent is not only possible but necessary to "further the movement and prepare a new generation of activists" (woodturtle). One feminist parenting blogger (Undercover in the Suburbs) commented, "I'm using my blog as a way to carve out an identity that is feminist and mother at the same time. I don't want to have to choose me versus motherhood."

FEMINIST PARENTING LITERATURE

We observed that feminist parenting bloggers, though not formally feminist scholars, engage with issues that gender scholars care about—such as systemic oppression and social privilege, gender socialization, hegemonic masculinity and femininity, activism and allyship, and equity. As such, these blogs are important sites to study everyday inequality.

Gender socialization is a rich field of research and is the focus of Emily Kane's qualitative research on the spectrum of parents who navigate "the gender trap." In *The Gender Trap*, Kane reveals how today's parents observe and participate in the gendering of their children, depending on how they viewed the origins, importance, and flexibility of gender. She describes two types of parents, called "innovators" and "resistors," who interrupt traditional gender norms, who recognize gender as a source of power, and who we consider to be feminist parents. Kane argues that conventional gender expectations are deeply entrenched and that there is great tension in attempting to undo them (201).

Kane's theories of gender socialization are supported by numerous studies on gender development. Children perceive gender very early, and once gender-related characteristics are recognized, children use them to make sense of the world and themselves (Katz 331; Fitzpatrick and McPherson 128). The need for social belonging can drive children to act in ways that identify them as male or female, and peers strongly police transgressions of gender roles (Martin and Ruble 67). By age five, many children also recognize that masculinity means power, which creates a hierarchy of gender (McGuffy and Rich 609).

Parents play an influential role in gender socialization. Repetition of fixed binaries and stereotypes by parents and popular culture contributes to the everyday policing of children's gender expression. Feminist parenting research has also explored how contemporary parents are also negotiating gender roles, maintaining (or not) work-family balance, and reacting to different parental leave policies. From this literature, questions emerge that the feminist blogosphere can answer. These include questions about how to approach parenting with feminist social justice ideals, how to build community among otherwise physically isolated feminist parents, and perhaps most importantly, how to model feminism for a new generation.

METHODS

The thirty-six feminist parenting blogs that we researched are connected to one another, either by mentioning others in a "blogroll" on their site through hyperlinks in blog posts or by discussions in comment sections. Because of these overt connections, we feel that these thirty-six blogs represent an online community, or a virtual feminist parenting subculture. Together, these sites provide us with an opportunity to research online community building and feminist activism.

We began our research in June 2013 by searching online for feminist parenting blogs. We focused on blogs over other social media websites because blogs appeared to better enable conversation among followers. Blogs themselves are based on an overriding theme, and blog-post comments sections can sustain pages of discussion. That said, blogs are not separate from other social media sites. Claims in the blogosphere travel through Facebook, Twitter, and other sites. We identified feminist parenting blogs through personal correspondence with feminist parenting researcher Emily Kane, reviews of parenting and feminist blog sites, and use of the Google search engine (using terms such as "feminist parenting," "gender justice parenting," "gender equality," etc.). We identified thirty-six applicable blogs that came up repeatedly in Google searches, many of which reference others in the sample.

Although not all bloggers were self-identified feminists, all of the bloggers we interviewed could be described as "resistors" or "innovators," or those who recognize and disrupt gender, according to Kane's research. Their blogs conveyed social justice themes, such as emphasizing gender equity in families, and many used terms, including commercialization, rape culture, gender equity, racial minority pride, gender nonconforming, and hegemonic masculinity. These terms are common parlance for gender scholars; therefore, we chose the term "feminist parenting bloggers" to describe the gender justice parenting blogs in this study. Because these blogs are publicly accessible and theme based, we chose to use their real account names rather than protect their identities with pseudonyms. We also gave our informants an opportunity to view a draft of this article before publication.

Content analysis involved coding blogs based on content, critical lenses, intended audiences, product reviews, personal or broad interest, traffic and media exposure, and blogger demographics. Common codes included community, gender, work, time, and privacy. Using this information, we created our own feminist parenting blog in July 2013: *Unconventional Kids! A Socially Aware Parenting Blog*. Creating this blog taught us how to build followers and community and become participant observers in the feminist parenting blogosphere. Then, we contacted all thirty-six bloggers by email and introduced ourselves as new bloggers and researchers interested in feminist parenting blogs. We included a questionnaire with five open-ended questions focused on goals and motivations for creating a blog as well as challenges and successes over time. A total of fourteen bloggers completed questionnaires, and six of them responded twice (once in 2013 and once in 2014), which allowed us to track changes over time.

One risk of doing research on social media is the quickly changing nature of the field. However, because our research lasted two years, we were able to track changes in bloggers and their blogs. This research captures presentations of self that are voluntarily shared with the public and are based in lived practices. However, that these daily weblogs are self-censored and socially constructed must be kept in mind. This chapter is organized around the most salient themes that emerged from content analysis and questionnaire data analysis. Studying these blogs helps to better understand the many complex and contested forms of contemporary feminism and feminist organizing.

FINDINGS

In this section we analyze how bloggers 1) do feminism in families; 2) counter isolation and build community online; 3) negotiate internal and external obstacles to online community; and 4) sustain their activism offline. The quotes highlighted below are taken primarily from blogger interviews (questionnaires).

Doing Feminism in Families

Roughly half of bloggers in this study identify as feminist parents, and although there are definite similarities in their descriptions of feminist parenting, there are also differences in emphasis—from valuing gender and difference, to teaching activism, and to modelling equity in a marriage. Blogger Mothering in the Margins writes, "My definition of feminist parenting also incorporates teaching children to be activists and not to be idle bystanders to discrimination. This does not necessarily mean that everyone must engage in formal activism but that we must encourage children to speak up against oppression when they witness it even if it does not directly affect them." Blogger Pigtail Pals and Ballcap Buddies write,

> I think a feminist parent is a parent who values the intrinsic worth of girls and women, teaches that value to their

children, teaches acceptance of the gender spectrum and LGBTQ communities, is sex positive and value positive body image and self love, who models a balanced/equitable relationship with their parenting partner, and who does not accept limiting gender stereotypes or harmful sexualization as the status quo for their family.

For many bloggers, good feminist parenting requires communicating strong and clear feminist values, including sending overt messages about the value of girls and women, promoting acceptance in the context of difference, modelling equity in the household, and taking a stand against harmful stereotypes.

In questionnaire responses, several bloggers discuss their personal growth as feminists that eventually fed into creating feminist families. For example, the blogger Feminist Fatherhood talks about how his wife and daughter strengthened his ideological development, and how the blog became a crucial step in envisioning and creating a different world for his daughter. He writes, "Becoming a father of a daughter really upped the ante for me as far as my dedication to feminist causes. My wife is a survivor of both DV [domestic violence] and SA [sexual assault] from a former relationship and I want to create a world in which my daughter doesn't have to deal with this sort of crap."

Through their answers, the bloggers describe how blog posts become spaces to grapple with negotiating feminism in combination with other important aspects of identity. Above, Feminist Fatherhood explores feminist parenting from the perspective of a man, a father, an activist, and a husband. The bloggers quoted below — self-defined as Arab-Muslim and Latina respectively —address their struggle as mothers in the face of difficult cultural and religious traditions. All envision their blogs as virtual spaces where they are able to engage intersecting identities. For example, blogger Wood Turtle writes, "There's an Arab/Muslim tradition of 'renaming yourself' after your first born that I've totally rejected. I refuse to be 'Umm Eryn' (mom of Eryn) because I'm 'K' and having a child suddenly does not automatically turn me into a be-all-end-all-mother. So when family or the community call me 'Umm Eryn' I ignore them." Similarly,

Viva la Feminista writes:

> Now that my daughter is eight, I'm long past the fawning posts of her infancy and when I write about mothering her, it's about all those screwed up decisions we have to make about raising girls, especially Latina girls in our world. I hope I still am achieving my goal of showing that feminists can be mothers and Latinas are feminists ... and that some of us are all three!

Like identity, feminist parenting can be messy and complex. Online, small acts of resistance become magnified, and bloggers may turn into facilitators of consciousness-raising groups, which invites commentary and conversation and, sometimes, enables readers to connect private troubles to public issues (Mills). The moment personal logs enter the social media domain, they can engage readers all over the world and, thus, go beyond the personal and the familial realm.

These feminist bloggers indicate that their primary goal is creating space to think through new parenting and identity challenges. They also seek social validation and paid-work opportunities. However, they also state that at the heart of feminist parenting blogging, there is a search for community. The next section addresses how online feminist parenting communities enable isolated feminist parents to connect to and participate in a larger feminist parenting movement.

Countering Isolation, Building Community

According to our respondents, the primary shared goal and desired outcome of feminist parenting bloggers is meaningful community. Most mention feeling alone, isolated, and/or excluded as feminist parents. Blogs are spaces where they can seek out personal and political support and, perhaps, enable a "personal is political" transformation among their readers. An experience that involves connection, community, and friendship is what defines success for these feminist parenting bloggers. In this way, blogging can create a consciousness-raising space, where making links between personal, public, or political realms is the norm. For example, blogger Blue Milk writes,

I am now convinced that feminists want very much to read about how other feminists are living their lives. There is a huge curiosity among us about the in's and out's of feminist lives. We don't have a lot of role models; we don't have a lot of traditions to follow.... Deep down I have this evangelist fantasy where I think many mothers can find their way to feminism through motherhood, so my blog is also a bit about that, opening the doors for people.

Similarly, Disney Princess Recovery writes:

Having a blog has connected me to so many others who are writing and asking the same questions. It reminds me that none of us is alone as we try to journey where we are. It has expanded my world in a wonderful invisible way. To get emails from students and professors and researchers and documentary filmmakers who are all diving in and exploring, is amazing.... I go back to when I began blogging and it was because I felt alone and kind of nuts in my actual world with the things I noticed. And in the online community, I find the opposite of that is true. It's a powerful tool.

Disney Princess Recovery and Blue Milk speak directly to how blogging moved them beyond isolated worlds, where they felt excluded because of their values and beliefs, to a sense of community, connection, and even leadership. In this larger online community context, the feminist social justice bloggers that we surveyed see themselves paving the way for new generations and "opening doors" for fellow feminists in the U.S. and globally. Feminist Fatherhood, for example, says:

I've actually received a lot of positive feedback from other dads in Europe and South America, and it's interesting to see how the concept of fathering within the context of feminism is becoming attractive to men on a global scale. That's the kind of movement we're going to need to create the radical cultural shift around gender issues that we need to be successful.

Community support (virtual or not) can be cathartic for bloggers, who feel isolated and excluded in their social worlds, as well as their readers. For example, the three bloggers below create community and cultural support for themselves and their families.

First the Egg morphed into an absolutely vital support network and community. I had an extremely unpleasant pregnancy, and suddenly my "Internet friends" were the only people other than my partner and midwife who really got what I was going through and why it mattered so much. During that period, some of my online relationships blossomed into really close friendships, and the blog temporarily served a new set of purposes in my life. (First the Egg)

My son's father is English, and we decided to move to my home country, the U.S., rather than his. Through my blogging (and my Twitter identity), I have had remarkable success connecting with feminists and feminist mothers from the UK. This has helped me share this aspect of his culture with him in a much more genuine and authentic way—their voices are a consistent part of how I parent my child. These women have also made a space for me, acknowledging that I am raising a British child outside of the UK and they have honoured my voice and our experience. (Our Feminist Playschool)

We've learned a lot about ourselves and our sons. We've learned that for the safety of our family, we may have to distance ourselves from certain types of people. We've learned who our real allies are—the people who will, no matter what, support us and join us as we take our journey and raise a gender nonconforming, possibly LGBTQ son. Most importantly, we've learned that we aren't alone.... I've built relationships with moms who travelled this path and are a little further down the road than I am and are now raising amazing young adults. (Raising My Rainbow)

As Raising My Rainbow points out, feminist community work may start with a broader vision of inclusion, but some "distancing" may be necessary in order to protect oneself and build sustainable alliances. Although community is an important aspect of feminist blogs, our respondents indicate that there are challenges to creating these connections.

Internal and External Obstacles to Community

Not all blogs succeed at building community. Some blogs may not capture readers for a variety of reasons, leading to reduced feedback. Other blogs—by virtue of the blogger's identity, radical ideas, or exclusionary language—can lead to feelings of exclusion, judgement, or discord among bloggers and their readers. This challenge can be seen in how these bloggers discuss the blurry line between being inclusive and exclusionary, radical and offensive. Mothering in the Margins writes, " Race, class, gender, sexuality, etc all should be addressed if not together then in turn. There has to be a balance of perspectives. I hate reading a blog and feeling completely left out when it is a subject that profoundly affects me." Similarly, Wood Turtle comments,

> My challenge about being heard in the feminist sphere is trying to balance my own ideals without offending my family's culture. But with so few Muslim feminists blogging, it's important to start these dialogues and to share our stories.

Feminist parenting bloggers struggle with many of the same issues as other feminist activists, including potential for community, internal discord, or virulent attacks from outside. Although feminist parenting bloggers see their Internet "genre" as separate from and sometimes in tension with general Internet feminism, one major obstacle all feminist online communities share is trolls, or Internet users who spread hatred and promote discord in online communities.

Danger of attacks by trolls and privacy concerns make blogging a risky activity, particularly when a blog site has feminism in its name or when it makes activism central to its aims. As Grauerholtz and Baker-Sperry remind us, the Internet allows for minorities, including trans people and feminists, to have a voice while, at the same time, it gives space to white supremacists and misogynists (290). Similarly, writing a feminist parenting blog opens the writer and his or her family up to public scrutiny by individuals who may not share similar viewpoints. The bloggers we interviewed are aware of these issues and attentive to their management. For example, Feminist Fatherhood writes, "Unfortunately, as I recently became a federal employee and had to undergo some intense background checks to secure employment I got paranoid that they would be monitoring my online presence, and flag me as a rabble rouser, and [I] haven't been posting as often as I should." And Pigtail Pals and Ballcap Buddies say, "I picked up a good rule from a fellow blogger that once my kids turn ten I would no longer share photos of them so that they could go through puberty and middle school with a bit of privacy. That is a tough space in life and having photos shared with tens of thousands of people most likely does not make it easier."

Trolling of feminist parenting blogs can be exceptionally threatening, graphic, and violent. The blogger Our Feminist Playschool found her posts shared on "hate" sites, which led to increased trolling, hateful commentary, and personal threats on her own blog. For bloggers who are threatened, the need to protect family and oneself becomes central, and it takes incredible perseverance to continue as a community leader. Offbeat Families writes, "The trolling of feminist parenting websites has gotten unbelievably vicious (even threatening) in recent years. This was not as bad when I was initially blogging, and I will definitely have to consider how I will approach dealing with trolls or if I will even allow comments going forward." Similarly, Princess Free Zone says, "You still get people who think this is insane, what I do. One guy had a ten minute YouTube rant about me. From Canada. When I saw it, there was a pit in my stomach—he could find me, easily. He could find where my daughter went to school. It's scary!"

Selections of privacy management strategies vary along with differences in bloggers' personalities, styles, and concerns. Often, feminist parenting bloggers start blogging during pregnancy and may slow down as their children age; many stop as their children reach preteen years and desire more privacy. However, several of the initial thirty feminist parenting bloggers stopped posting blog entries before their children reached that stage. Although we do not have access to their reasons for stopping, the issues of privacy and trolling may have been contributing factors. Other bloggers state that they addressed the threat of trolls by self-censoring to avoid conflicts in their "real" lives or to protect themselves and their families. Thus, both external threats (such as Internet trolls) and internal threats (such as exclusionary posts from other blogs) can threaten the larger community by making bloggers feel uncomfortable or unsafe. In this way, the world of feminist blogging mirrors many social justice activist groups that face challenges from outside harassment and "call outs" by their activist community. For those feminist bloggers who do persevere despite obstacles, the effects of their activism on and offline can be substantial.

Sustaining Activism Offline

From changing personal views, to shifting critical public discourse, and to creating local nonvirtual support groups, feminist parenting blogs have made tangible differences in their worlds and beyond. For example, blogger Princess Free Zone pitched an idea for a new kid-friendly TV character to Nickelodeon and formed the Brave Girls Alliance to continue to push for change. Mamafesto plans to piggyback on a popular social justice and reproductive rights conference with a small feminist parenting conference of her own. Raising My Rainbow launched *Rainbows at Play*, "an online community that connects families raising gender nonconforming kids so they can playdate and find fierceness in numbers." Pigtail Pals was one of five feminist bloggers we followed to receive a book offer because of a successful blog. Her children's book and clothing line are continuing the work of the feminist parenting movement in new and diverse communities. Beyond creating virtual communities, some bloggers foster physical safe spaces, both for their children and themselves, in the form of playdates, conferences, and writers groups. By being feminist leaders in their local communities, nationally, and online, their community-building impact is magnified.

Although blogging may have been one step in community building, feminist parenting bloggers have shown how important offline activism can be in terms of envisioning structural change. The transition to offline activism is particularly crucial as media platforms shift and change.

CONCLUSIONS

The feminist parenting movement builds from the success of mommy blogs and mainstream feminism to explicitly address issues that affect mothers, children, and families in particular. Feminist parenting blogs are important sites to study everyday equality and social attempts at dismantling rigid gender roles. These bloggers are activists employing consciousness-raising tactics to foster community and social change. Parents who are resistors and innovators when it comes to gendering their children may find that regular social media contact with feminist blogging and social media communities provides sustained support for their nonconventional childraising efforts. If gender is to be undone for future generations, enabling parent activists to connect with one another is a crucial step.

At times, however, this community neglects to address race and class issues, possibly because of the particular cohort of college-educated individuals that is predominant in this group. Our research shows that discussions of racial and class inequality are still lacking in many of these activist blogs, especially those written by middle- or upper-class white women. Much like white feminism offline, online feminisms reproduce privilege in nonreflexive ways. In fact, we found few feminist parenting blogs that engaged with larger social justice questions about capitalism, racism, religion, or the environment. For example, the #*solidarityisforwhitewomen* hashtag trended internationally in feminist circles in 2013 to raise awareness about white privilege and noninclusive feminisms, but only three of the feminist parenting bloggers we followed engaged or responded to this media movement. These mostly white, middle class, twenty-to-thirty-something millennial generation parents have been shaped by third-wave feminism and exposed to women's studies as a discipline. They became parents during a time when online blogging was becoming a new platform for community and discovery, and they used that opportunity to start a movement. Their online feminist parenting blogs helped start a new era of mindful, conscious parenting. Our research has captured a moment in this movement, but it is a moment with a lasting impact.

The Internet is a fast-paced and quickly changing place, and the first generation of feminist parenting bloggers may be moving on, as their children grow up. Almost one-third of the bloggers we followed had stopped posting by 2014; some of them explicitly retired, whereas others simply disappeared. We did not find any feminist parenting blogs starting after the year 2012, so it appears that there is not a balance of incoming and outgoing blogs. These trends reveal that the peak of feminist parenting blogs may have already passed and that the feminist parenting community may be moving on to other forms of communication—such as Facebook, Twitter, and Instagram—especially as busy parents shift from computers to smartphones. When asked about this, feminist parenting bloggers argue that the online feminist community is not disappearing, it is just changing platforms as the mobile Internet infrastructure expands. Although the format of the online feminist parenting community may be shifting from blogging to other social media, it seems that the community itself is still gaining strength and revolutionary potential. Whether or not blogs are still the main platform is debatable. Our hope is that conversations about feminist parenting, mediated or not, proliferate into the future.

WORKS CITED

Aronowitz, Nona Willis. "Raising the Baby Question." *Nation,* The Nation Company LLC, 12 May 2009. www.thenation.com/article/raising-baby-question/. Accessed 17 July 2014.

Fitzpatrick, Maureen J., and Barbara J. McPherson. "Coloring within the Lines: Gender Stereotypes in Contemporary Coloring Books." *Sex Roles*, vol. 62, no. 1, 2010, pp. 127-138.

Friedman, May, and Shana Calixte, editors. *Mothering and Blogging: The Radical Act of the MommyBlog*. Demeter Press, 2011.

Grauerholz, L., and L. Baker-Sperry. "Feminist Research in the Public Domain: Risks and Recommendations." *Gender & Society*, vol. 21, no. 2, 2007, pp. 272-294.

Kane, Emily W. *The Gender Trap: Parents and the Pitfalls of Raising*

Boys and Girls. New York University Press, 2012.

Katz, Phyllis A. "Raising Feminists." *Psychology of Women Quarterly* vol. 20, no. 3, 1996, pp. 323-340.

Lopez, Lori K. "The Radical Act of 'Mommy Blogging': Redefining Motherhood through the Blogosphere." *New Media & Society*, vol. 11, no. 2009, pp. 729-747.

Martin, Carol L., and Diane Ruble. "Children's Search for Gender Cues: Cognitive Perspectives on Gender Development." *Current Directions in Psychological Science*, vol. 13, 2004, pp. 67-70.

McGuffy, C. Shawn, and B. Lindsay Rich. "Playing in the Gender Transgression Zone: Race, Class, and Hegemonic Masculinity in Middle Childhood." *Gender & Society*, vol. 13, no. 5, 1999, pp. 608-627.

Mills, C. Wright. *The Sociological Imagination*. Oxford University Press, 1959.

Nathman, Avital Norman. "The Femisphere: More Mama Bloggin'." *The Mamafesto*, WordPress, 16 Apr. 2012, themamafesto. wordpress.com/2012/04/. Accessed 31 July 2013.

Pippert, Julia. "A Mum and a Feminist." *The Guardian*, Guardian News and Media Limited, 22 May 2009. www.theguardian. com/commentisfree/2009/may/22/feminism-blogging. Accessed 17 July 2014.

Epilogue

MATERNAL SUBJECTIVITIES ARE FLUID constructions. These identities are created and recreated as women negotiate the various challenges and possibilities that characterize the transitions of motherhood. How women come to experience their identity as mothers is directly related to the cultural mediation of their maternal experience. In the preindustrial era, this mediation was generally enacted through female relationships within particular geographical and cultural contexts; however, the disembedding of identity through the mobilization of both peoples and culture has threatened experiential ways of knowing and more authentic expressions of selfhood, particularly those related to maternal practice.

As is made clear by the chapters in this volume, for mothers, community interaction has shifted in appearance but not in importance. With the advent of the digital age and the increasing availability of both mobile digital devices and Internet access, unprecedented numbers of women from all demographics are accessing social media to communicate their experience of motherhood and seek validation and support for that experience. Mothers have taken to Facebook, blogs, Twitter, as well as a myriad of popular mothering sites to understand and contextualize their mothering. It is important to note, however, that communication through social media does not simply represent an exchange of ideas but rather a reciprocal and collaborative reconstruction of the meaning of maternal experience that has the power to signify beyond the digital sphere.

Social media has become a critical tool in women's negotiation of constructed meanings of motherhood. In a reciprocal relationship, mommy bloggers write to advance particular performances and narratives of mothering; in turn, audiences consume these narratives as they search for the meaning of their own mothering story. Whether blogs celebrate the ideology of intensive parenting, document the reality of maternal experience, or confess parenting "fails," all contribute to a host of narratives of maternal being that sometimes reinforce oppressive ideologies and sometimes work to liberate mothers from dominant cultural narratives that inscribe maternal identity. Social media—both its virtual spaces and the consumption of identities as they are constructed and actively negotiated within these spaces—has a potentially powerful and lasting impact on reconstructed meanings of motherhood as well as the lived performance of maternity.

Beyond identity construction and negotiation, online communities have become vital sources of maternal support. Facebook pages, discussion boards, and sites dedicated to particular maternal challenges are virtual gathering places for mothers struggling with breastfeeding, postpartum mood disorders, traumatic birth experiences, cultural dislocation, and a host of other parenting issues. In these communities, the traditional voice of the expert is often replaced by voices of experience. Here mothers find both the informational and emotional support that they need to overcome maternal hardship. Because of the myths of maternal perfection and the supposed intuitive nature of motherhood, new mothers often find it difficult to reach out for support; however, online communities offer access to service without the exposure that in-person support entails. As well, convenience and availability, in addition to advances such as the simulation of experience through avatars, suggests that virtual communities will continue to play a critical role in mother's search for educational resources and personal support.

In addition to support, mothers often seek like-minded mothers online to explore possibilities for resistance. Although some sites and pages may shame mothers by reinforcing intensive parenting ideals and by openly critiquing mothers who do not uphold them, there is a thriving network of online communities dedicated to conscious resistance to normative expectations and roles traditionally associated with the institution of motherhood. Feminist blogs about motherhood continue a dialogue about oppressive cultural myths that deny mothers a sense of autonomy in their own maternal practice. Such sites advocate active participation in the project of liberating the performance of mothering from cultural scripts that obscure women's critical perception and maternal agency. Through a challenge to conventional voices and exploration of diversity, these sites celebrate the figure of the "mother outlaw" and open possibilities for authenticity through mothering and social action beyond the confines of the "mamasphere."

Ultimately, although the experience of community continues to evolve in various virtual formats, mothers' needs within their communities remain much the same: mothers seek resonance in the form of affirmation of their choices and identity; they seek both informational and emotional support; and, they seek alternatives and genuine opportunities to critically examine and reclaim their role. This collection details the manner in which all of these functions are continuously evolving in various online communities. Given the contemporary reality of disembedded and commodified identity, virtual spaces allow mothers to actively negotiate their mothering journey with the support of other women who serve as virtual guides and educators in a world of maternal experience that is both daunting and unfamiliar. The implications of access to and availability of this kind of support are undeniable. Indeed, mothers' perceptions of self-efficacy often hinge on the affirmation and support generally provided by peers and professionals. Women who explore online communities towards the projects of affirmation, education, support, and resistance generally find a supportive network of mothers willing to share experiential knowledge of mothering. In this way, social media functions as a conduit for mentorship and self-directed learning that aids the development of maternal confidence and, thereby, promotes self-actualization. Through its various portals, then, mothers are liberated to engage and reconstruct cultural narratives of maternity and, in doing so, reclaim the agency required to practice mothering in ways that invite wellness and empowerment.

About the Contributors

Lorin Basden Arnold is a family communication and gender scholar. Her recent scholarly work has primarily related to understandings and enactments of motherhood and appeared in recent Demeter editions, including *Intensive Mothering: The Cultural Contradictions of Modern Motherhood* and *What's Cooking Mom? Narratives about Food and Family*. She is the provost and vice-president for academic affairs at the State University of New York, New Paltz.

Kirsti Cole is an associate professor of rhetoric, composition, and literature at Minnesota State University. She teaches in the teaching writing graduate certificate program and in the communication and composition graduate program. She has published articles in *Feminist Media Studies*, *College English*, *Harlot*, and *thirdspace*, and her collection *Feminist Challenges or Feminist Rhetorics* was published in 2014.

Tess Cumpstone is a recent graduate of Colgate University, where she majored in women's studies and minored in peace and conflict Studies. Tess hopes to pursue a master's degree in women and gender studies and is interested in the function of self-representation as an act of resistance, catharsis, and restoration for survivors of oppression.

Jocelyn Craig is a feminist mother of two young daughters and a graduate student in women's studies at San Diego State University. She is currently working on her thesis on motherhood as a site of the development of feminist consciousness for feminist-identified single mothers.

Amy Cross is an interdisciplinary PhD student at the University of Maine. Her research regarding the effects of the avatar in virtual learning environments stems from her experience in the virtual world where she found that as an avatar, she was much more confident and engaged than in her physical world. Amy is a single mother of two boys, aged twelve and twenty-four. She lives in Bangor Maine, on the banks of the Penobscot River.

Troy D. Glover is a professor in the Department of Recreation and Leisure Studies and director of the Healthy Communities Research Network at the University of Waterloo. Focused primarily within an urban context, his research explores the transformative possibilities of leisure, tourism, and sport in the advancement of community, place, and social capital.

Anitra Goriss-Hunter lectures in the fields of education and gender in the Faculty of Education and Arts at Federation University, Ballarat, Australia. Anitra's doctoral thesis, *Wired and Dangerous: Maternal Bodies in Cyber(cultural)space*, was awarded the prestigious Australian Women's and Gender Studies PhD Award. Her research areas include cybercultures, representations of maternal bodies, inclusive education, and preservice teacher education.

Stephanie C. Kennedy is an assistant professor in the School of Social Work at the University of Connecticut. Her research examines the intersection of trauma and serious mental health issues for institutionalized women. Her research goals include investigating the theoretical assumptions that inform current best practices and service provision.

Meika Loe is professor of sociology and women's studies at Colgate University, where she teaches about aging, gender, culture, and medicine. Meika is the author of *Aging Our Way: Lessons for Living from 85 and Beyond* and *The Rise of Viagra: How the Little Blue Pill Changed Sex in America*, and is co-editor of

Technogenarians: Studying Health and Illness Through an Aging, Science, and Technology Lens.

BettyAnn Martin is a doctoral candidate in educational sustainability at Nipissing University, North Bay, ON. She is an educator, doula, mother, and postpartum support coordinator with PSI (Postpartum Support International). Her research interests include the cultural mediation of maternal experience and identity as well as the educational and therapeutic aspects of shared personal narrative.

Susan B. Miller is a recent graduate of Colgate University, where she majored in women's studies and peace and conflict studies. Susan is hoping to gain international experience working for women's access to health and justice in postconflict communities. She is also hoping to pursue a master's degree.

Kate Orton-Johnson is a senior lecturer in Sociology at the University of Edinburgh, UK. Her research interests focus on digital cultures and digital leisure, and the ways in which cultures of technology and technologies of culture shape our social lives.

Diana C. Parry is a professor in the Department of Recreation and Leisure Studies at the University of Waterloo. Utilizing a feminist lens, Diana's research explores the personal and political links between women's leisure and women's health, broadly defined. Diana's research privileges women's standpoints and aims to create social change and enact social justice by challenging the medical model of scholarship.

Valerie R. Renegar is an associate professor of communication studies at Southwestern University. Her research centres on contemporary feminist rhetoric and rhetorical theory. Her work has been published in *Hypatia, the Western Journal of Communication, Southern Communication Journal, the Howard Journal of Communications, Environmental Communication,* and *Philosophy and Rhetoric.*

Amy Barron Smolinski is the executive director for Mom2Mom

Global, a breastfeeding support network for military families. An advanced lactation consultant, army wife, and breastfeeding mother living in Germany, she holds an MA from Union Institute & University, where her thesis explored re-emerging Sacred Feminine manifestations in the lives of contemporary women.

Tara Stamm is an assistant professor of sociology at Virginia Commonwealth University. Her current research spotlights the experiences and depictions of young mothers, the importance of emerging mixed-methodological techniques, and intersections between gender, education, and media in popular culture.

Bronwen L. Valtchanov is a doctoral candidate in Recreation and Leisure Studies at the University of Waterloo. Diverse feminist theoretical approaches inform her qualitative research, which explores women's negotiations of identity transitions, including motherhood. Bronwen's research aims to elucidate the complexities of women's lived experiences and engage possibilities for social justice.

Leah Williams Veazey is a doctoral student at the University of Sydney, Australia. Her research focuses on migrant mothers and online communities, with related interests in feminism, intersectionality, and digital sociology. She is also an online community manager and migrant mother of two.

Casey Yu is an assistant professor and Chinese American expatriate at North South University in Dhaka, Bangladesh. She is also a photographer and mother of three kids, who have benefited greatly from their mother's mothers of honor. Her work investigates how women who have Caesarean births use camera-phone photography to gain and share knowledge.